August 12, 1987
Skipton
Elizabeth Clifford Yocom

PROUD NORTHERN LADY

PROUD NORTHERN LADY

Lady Anne Clifford
1590~1676

Martin Holmes

PHILLIMORE

First published 1975 by
PHILLIMORE & CO. LTD.
Shopwyke Hall, Chichester, Sussex, England

CORRECTED REPRINT 1984

ISBN 0 85033 225 7

Printed and bound in Great Britain by
BILLINGS BOOK PLAN
Worcester, England

CONTENTS

LIST OF PLATES

Chapter One

CLIFFORD OF CUMBERLAND

Proud northern lord, Clifford of Cumberland
III Henry VI, V, ii

IN THE YEAR 1590, two important things happened to George Clifford, third Earl of Cumberland. One of them was an outstanding public honour, the other a private event which must have come to him as a major disappointment. Both are worth considering for their effect on him and on others.

The first was his appointment to the post of Champion to his sovereign, Queen Elizabeth, in succession to the elderly Sir Henry Lee. Like her father Henry VIII, Elizabeth enjoyed the splendours and excitements of the tilt-yard, but unlike him she could do so only as a spectator, not as a combatant. By way of atoning for this disability and identifying herself, as closely as might be, with the royal sport, she contrived to take part in it by deputy, nominating an official champion who would wear her badge or colours and do battle in her name. To be selected for such an office was a real guarantee of quality, for the Queen was a shrewd judge of such matters, and could be counted on to choose the best that could be had, so it was natural for the chosen champion to equip himself for the jousting and pageantry in a style worthy of the great lady whom he represented. A famous miniature by Nicholas Hilliard shows Cumberland in armour decorated with golden stars and partly concealed by a light blue surcoat bordered with gold. He is unhelmed, but wears a tall, broad-brimmed hat turned up fore and aft and clasped with an ornament that at first sight looks like a cockade, but is seen, on examination, to be a lady's glove with the short cuff turned back flat against the fingers. The Queen's Champion is wearing the Queen's favour for all to see.

This star-patterned armour appears in other portraits of Cumberland, but cannot now be traced. He had another suit, however, also associated with his office and still in existence. Like the armour already described, it was made in the royal workshops at Greenwich, but instead of stars its engraved and gilded ornamentation embodies the Tudor rose, the lily of France and the initial of Elizabeth's name. For many years it stood in Appleby Castle, and though it is now in the Metropolitan Museum of Art in New York, a contemporary record of it, in the pattern-book of the Greenwich workshops, is still preserved in the Victoria and Albert Museum. This volume illustrates in detail the decoration of the armour itself and the number of extra pieces, to suit the different requirements of the tilt-yard or the field, that make up the elaborate 'garniture'.

And, like the armour, its wearer was fully qualified for practical service overseas as well as for sporting events at home. He was renowned as a valiant and enterprising sea-captain, organising ventures that were partly exploration and at times something very like piracy. Gorgeous and prodigal in his pageantry at home when the occasion called for display, he was never one to shirk hardship or privation at sea, but readily shared, at need, the labours and short rations of his men, just as Drake had done before him. He had commanded the *Elizabeth Bona-venture* against the great Armada in 1588, and in the year of his appointment as Champion he stormed Fayal in the Azores and dismantled its Spanish fortifications. The earldom of Cumberland was a comparatively recent one, having been created only in 1522, and the Cliffords were in fact a long-established *Westmorland* family, but it is significant that in 1592 or thereabouts Shakespeare should have found it worth while to present an earlier Clifford in a way that would well suggest the current Champion. In the *Second Part of King Henry VI*, Lord Clifford appears as the boy-king's representative in battle, first against Jack Cade and his rebels and then,

with the beginning of the Wars of the Roses, against the
Plantagenet house of York. His name is the first word in
the first battle-scene, and is associated at once with the
title borne by his descendant, in the lines

> Clifford of Cumberland, 'tis Warwick calls! . . .
> Clifford, I say, come forth and fight with me!
> Proud northern lord, Clifford of Cumberland,
> Warwick is hoarse with calling thee to arms!

The association of Clifford with Cumberland at such a
moment would have more than alliteration to recommend
it. The playgoing public at the Theatre or the Curtain
would usually take a lively interest in social and sporting
events as well. To them, there was a real Clifford of
Cumberland, and everyone knew what, and whom, he
stood for. Warwick's challenge to such a man, by such
a name, had a suggestion of rebellion against the throne
itself, and Clifford's death at the hands of York—the first
death in all the confused battle-scenes of that play and its
successor—would appear as the initial act of violence
against the Lord's Anointed that set off the whole cycle
of bloodshed, misery and revenge.

Yet, even at this height of his swelling fortune, there
was matter for frustration and bitterness. The great
landowner of the north had won himself renown far
beyond the bounds of his own estates. He was now a
splendid and popular figure at Court and overseas,
loved and applauded by his followers and high in the
favour of his Queen. It was a fine heritage, one might
say, to pass on to his descendants, but there was no
certainty, by then, who would inherit it. Of Cumberland's
two sons, the elder had died in 1589 at the age of five and
a half, and his little brother, 18 months younger, was
already failing, and was soon to follow him. At the end of
January 1590, in the Yorkshire castle of Skipton-in-Craven,
Lady Cumberland gave birth to their last and only surviving
child—and it was a girl. They called her Anne.

Lord and Lady Cumberland had been fond of each
other since childhood. He had succeeded to the earl-

dom as a boy, and had been a ward of the Court in consequence. Elizabeth had granted the guardianship of his person and the administration of his property to Francis Russell, second Earl of Bedford, and at the age of 19 he had been married to Bedford's daughter Margaret. Many of his letters to her are still extant, having been carefully preserved by her and handed down to her daughter Anne, and it is clear from them that the marriage was one of genuine affection, independent of the policy that had lain behind it. Now, however, circumstances began to put that affection under increasingly heavy strain. Little Lord Clifford died in May 1591, while his father was abroad on one of his privateering expeditions, and as time went on, it must have become clear that there would be no more sons to inherit the earldom and the estates. Lady Cumberland's patient, careful disposition inclined her always to examine her circumstances and resources, make sure what they were and order her life accordingly. Her husband, on the other hand, was all for improving matters by bold, wild enterprises that were admittedly challenges to fortune. His Court appointment would encourage this feeling as a matter of course by providing him with a fashionable and admiring audience, and it is not surprising that husband and wife now drifted further and further apart. Some of the privateering ventures were successful, but this was not enough to counterbalance the fact that all of them were expensive, and the same could be said of his gambles at home, over what Lady Anne was later to summarise as 'horse-racing, tilting, shooting, bowling-matches and all such expensive sports'. We can see in this prodigality not only the expression of the Earl's natural instincts but a more and more frantic attempt to make up on the sporting roundabouts what was being lost on the privateering swings.

It was not an unusual state of affairs at that time. The Court of Elizabeth had become a place in which many a fortune could be made by the Queen's favour, or lost by unavailing attempts to win it. After the religious anxieties of Mary's reign, and the political uncertainties that had gone before it under the ambitious governors of Edward VI, and before that again, the general unease and apprehension in the last years of his father, the new Queen's accession had brought with it a return to the feeling of relief and joyous exuberance characteristic of the old days when Henry VIII was young. Men spent, lent, gave, borrowed and wagered, with energy and enthusiasm and sometimes with success. For many, however, the end was disappointment and eventual bankruptcy.

Shakespeare has depicted the process in the first three acts of *Timon of Athens,* and there are suggestions of it in *Richard II,* notably in the famous deathbed speech of John of Gaunt. This is remembered and justly honoured for its fine panegyric upon England, but we are apt to overlook the dramatic point that meant so much to the Elizabethans. What cuts the dying man to the heart is the knowledge that the King has raised money by pledging his heritage this way and that, 'like to a tenement or pelting farm'. Land, especially inherited land, was at once a great possession and a great responsibility, and a landowner owed something to the estates from which he drew his revenues.

With the practical certainty that he would have no more sons, Cumberland took a drastic step to secure his estates and fulfil, as he saw them, his responsibilities. In 1605 he made a will leaving practically all of them to his younger brother Francis (who would naturally inherit his earldom) and to his heirs male, with the proviso that failing such heirs, the property was to come back to his daughter Anne. Francis was well-to-do, and would have less difficulty in keeping things together than an heiress in her 'teens, and to the hard-pressed Earl this move appeared a just and reasonable way of dealing with the problem. What he had overlooked was the awkward fact that it was not entirely legal. By a deed drawn up in the reign of Edward II, nearly three centuries before, the great northern estates were entailed in the direct line from parent to child, even if

that child should be a daughter. It was all very well for
Lord Cumberland to ensure that Lady Anne should inherit the property if the male line failed; it ought not,
in law, to have been left away at all, and very soon she
knew it.

Meanwhile, various important things had been happening. Little Anne had been brought up to Court, where she
had been, in her own words, 'much beloved by that
Renowned Queene Elizabeth'. In those days she promised
well to be an heiress and a beauty, and it was intended
that she should be appointed in due course to a post in
the Privy Chamber, but in March 1603, when Lady Anne
was 13 years old, the old Queen died, and everything was
changed. To her disappointment, the little girl was
considered too young to take her turn as a watcher at
the royal lying-in-state, and too small to walk in the
funeral procession as her mother did, but she duly
'stood in the church at *Westminster* to see the solemnities
performed'. When the new King came south from Scotland,
Lord Cumberland was one of the peers who went to meet
him and escort him on his way, and when he reached
Theobalds Park (not in those days a royal possession, but
soon to be acquired from the Cecils in exchange for
Hatfield House) Lady Cumberland and her daughter went
with several others to get a sight of him. Incidentally,
they noticed that the Court was not kept as it had been
in Elizabeth's time, as they all picked up lice from sitting
in the room of Sir Thomas Erskine, who had succeeded
Sir Walter Ralegh as Captain of the Guard.

By this time the Cumberlands were no longer living
together. The Earl still visited his wife and daughter
occasionally, and paid their living expenses in Lady
Cumberland's house at Clerkenwell, but it would seem,
from a note of Lady Anne's, that he was now the lover
of 'a lady of quality' whom his daughter does not name.
An awkward situation arose when he gave a banquet
at Grafton Regis in Northamptonshire and lavishly
entertained the King and the newly-arrived Queen. From
Lady Anne's memorandum of her early life it appears

that she and her mother were in the Queen's train during this part of the royal journey, and she specifically mentions that 'At this time of the King's being at *Grafton,* my Mother was there, but not held as mistress of the house, by reason of the difference between my Lord and her, which was grown to a great height'. It is worth noticing that there is no mention of anyone else's having been called upon to act as hostess. The late Dr. G. C. Williamson, in his book on Lady Anne, suggests that Lady Cumberland's place had been taken by 'her own sister, in all probability', but had it been so, Lady Anne would almost certainly have mentioned the fact. If, on the other hand, Cumberland had established the unnamed 'lady of quality' or some other mistress, the scandal would have been open, and likely to reflect upon his royal guests if they accepted the position without comment or objection. This would have entirely defeated Cumberland's purpose—the not unnatural one of doing everything possible to earn the favour of his new sovereign.

There may well be a far simpler explanation. The running of a great house like Grafton would be an elaborate business at all times, and would be carried out by a large staff of persons of all ranks permanently retained to deal with it. George Cavendish, gentleman-usher to Wolsey, has left us a detailed account of the establishment maintained by the great Cardinal, and the same thing, on a smaller scale, was characteristic of any Elizabethan or Jacobean nobleman's house in the succeeding years. Moreover, there is nothing to suggest that Lady Cumberland had been expected at Grafton. She and her daughter had gone to meet the new Queen Consort, who was on her way down from Scotland. They joined the royal procession in Northamptonshire, and moved on with it, by way of Althorp, to Hatton Ferrers, where it was met by the King, and the whole Court then moved to Grafton on its way to Windsor, but there is no suggestion, or even likelihood, that the Queen and her ladies knew beforehand, in any detail, what had been decided for their next stopping-place. Cumberland would have made all his arrangements as if he were a bachelor or widower; it would have been impossible for his wife to step in and assume control of the whole complicated organisation without warning, while to avoid the visit, by asking the Queen's leave to absent herself from Court, would indicate only too plainly that she and her husband had seriously fallen out. With her customary patience and good judgement she did the best thing possible, and avoided all occasion for criticism, but for the little girl of 13 the episode must have been a disappointment, and what was worse, a slight to the mother she adored.

Mother and daughter remained in the Queen's train, attending her to Windsor—where the Garter feast was kept with great splendour—and to Hampton Court. Lady Anne's memorandum records that her mother had 'to attend the King about the business between my Father and her', and it appears that the Earl was independently a suitor to the King for some property in Cumberland, for which he later claimed to have had 'his Majesty's princely word and promise', so that they occasionally met, but with mutual distaste. Though they themselves were not on speaking terms, the Earl would take enough notice of his daughter to speak to her 'in a slight fashion' and give her his blessing, but that was all.

He had enough thought for her to consider the important question of her marriage. If the estates in the north were to go to his brother, as he was planning, his daughter must be otherwise provided for, and two years later, when she was 15, he was obviously discussing the question with her. A letter written by her to her mother in 1605 says that 'I have had a great deal of talk with my Lord about that matter you know of, for that match, and my Lord hath promised me that there shall nothing pass for any match whatsoever, but that your consent should be asked as a chief matter'. The will which caused so much trouble had been made four months earlier, and though little Lady Anne was not the great heiress that she should have been, she was a young woman with expectations, and with very good family

connections. Her father's will had manifestly wronged
her in one way, but he would naturally feel that it was
possible to make it up to her in another, and he seems to
have lost little time in setting about it. His daughter was
summoned to Grafton and spent a month there with
him, much to her mother's reluctance. Her letter suggests
that the Earl was less peremptory than he had been,
and was trying to show some belated consideration for
his wife's feelings. At the end of August he took his
daughter down on her way to Kent, where Lady Cumberland was staying, and took leave of her on Greenwich
Heath. We know nothing more of his plans for that pro-
jected match, for they were cut short by his unexpected
illness, and by the end of October he was dead.

He died in 'the Duchy house' by the *Savoy*, the most
famous, perhaps, of the great riverside palaces of the
Strand. His wife and daughter were with him at the
end, and a touching letter to his 'sweet and dear Meg'
shows the depths of his affection, in spite of all the
wrongs done to her, and makes his last requests, 'which
as ever thou lovest me living, so I pray thee perform
for me being dead'. First she is not 'to offend God in
grieving too much at this His disposing of me', and,
further, he begs her to 'take as I have meant, in kindness,
the course I have set down for the disposing of my
estate' which he was sure he had done in her own best
interests and those of the family. There is a pathetic
appeal for her not to think too hardly of his brother,
to whom she is doing less than justice, and a final plea
that their daughter may be brought up 'not to delight
in worldly vanities, which I too well know to be the
baits to draw her out of the Heavenly Kingdom'.

He died in the firm, though quite illogical, belief that
his brother's son would have no male issue, and that
the estates, preserved by his brother's care, would come
to his daughter in the end. So they did, but she had
to wait for them, and on occasion fight for them, for
nearly 40 years.

Chapter Two

THE HEIRESS AND HER HERITAGE

This worm-eaten hold of ragged stone
II Henry IV, Induction

IN THAT LAST APPEAL for more kindly consideration of his younger brother, the dying Lord Cumberland had overlooked two things of importance. One was the fact that that brother's 'sweet nature' would make it all the easier for a less accommodating character to dominate him, and the other was the possibility that his and his son's stewardship of the Westmorland estates might turn out to be a long one. George Clifford was dying at 47; his younger brother, Francis, on the other hand, lived to be nearly 82, and for much of that time he was influenced by the more forceful personality of his son Henry, who eventually became the fifth and last Earl of Cumberland, but held the title for only two years and left no son to succeed him. It seems more than likely that the careful husbandry of both men, and the strong business instincts of the younger one, did a very great deal to repair the fortunes of the estate. This was what the testator had intended, but it did not alter the irregularity of the bequest, or smooth matters over for the two women who were kept out of their inheritance.

The great estates in Yorkshire passed to the new earl on his brother's death, but the dowager Lady Cumberland's jointure had been settled upon her for her lifetime, by Act of Parliament, in 1593, and covered the Westmorland property, with its four castles of Appleby, Brougham, Brough and Pendragon. Most of these were in considerable disrepair. Appleby had been deliberately dismantled by its owner during the 'Rising in the North' of 1569, to prevent its occupation by the rebels while he was on duty at Carlisle. Pendragon had been burned by the Scots, and Brough by a casual fire. Brougham alone seems to have been kept regularly habitable. When William Camden, greatest of Elizabethan antiquaries, visited the neighbourhood at the turn of the century, he took note of all four places for *Britannia,* his elaborate county-by-county survey of the British Isles. An English translation from Camden's Latin, by Philemon Holland, was published in 1610, and gives us accordingly a fair impression of the county as it was at the time of Lord Cumberland's death. In the northern part, in which the Clifford estates lay, Camden found traces of Roman building and administration. He made numerous identifications, real or imaginary, with towns and stations mentioned in the *Antonine Itinerary,* but what seems to have impressed him most was the wildness and desolation that had succeeded the days of Roman prosperity. The very name of the county he derives from the fact that 'such barren places, which cannot easily by the painfull labour of the husbandman bee brought to fruitfulnesse, the Northern Englishmen call Moores'. Appleby, the county town, is 'in a pleasant site, encompassed for the most part with the river *Eden*: but so sclenderly inhabited, and the building so simple, that were it not that by reason of the antiquity it had deserved to be counted the chiefe towne of the shire, and to have Sessions and *Assises* kept in the castle, which is the common goale for malefactours, it would be little better than a village'. Brough, likewise, 'is decaied and become a small poore village fensed with a little Fortresse', while Pendragon Castle 'hath nothing left unto it unconsumed by time, besides the bare name, and an heape of stones'. Alluding to the Roman station of Brovoniacum, he says 'The beauty and buildings of this towne, although time hath consumed, yet the name remaineth almost untouched, for wee call it *Brougham',* and he makes no mention of the castle at all, presumably because it was still habitable and inhabited, and counted, from his point of view, as a house in current use, and not a monument of decayed antiquity.

To Westmorland, then, Lady Cumberland went in 1607, with the 17-year-old Lady Anne, who was now paying her first visit to the county which was to mean so much to her. They visited all four castles, but made Appleby their headquarters. The dismantling of the castle in the 1569 rising had been aimed at making it unsuitable for defence. The lead would have been stripped from the roofs, and a good deal of the timber removed for other purposes, but some of the residential part must still have been serviceable at Assize time, and 'malefactours' could still be lodged in the lowest storey of the Keep. Above all, the castle was in a market town, which would do much to compensate for a certain amount of discomfort in accommodation. Provisions could be obtained to an extent not possible at Brougham or in the 'small poore village' of Brough, and at Pendragon there was nothing at all.

The relation between Appleby and its castle was a peculiar one. Camden's account of the town as 'little better than a village' goes on with a piece of description that picks out the main features and shows how much of its character it has preserved through the three and a half centuries since Philemon Holland's words were written.

> For, all the beauty of it lieth in one broad street, which from North to South riseth with an easie ascent of the hill: in the upper part whereof standeth the castle aloft, environed wholy almost with the river. In the nether end of it is the church, and thereby a schoole, which Robert *Langton* and Miles *Spencer,* Doctors of the law founded; the Maister whereof is Reginald *Bainbrige,* a right learned man who governeth the same with great commendation; and who of his courtesie hath exemplified for me many antique inscriptions, and brought some hither into his garden.

The town's expansion on its outskirts has not greatly affected this description. The essential character of Appleby still lies in the wide sweep of Boroughgate, rising from the church and market-place to the castle gates at the top of the hill. This is a modern entrance, we must remember; in Lady Anne's time, and for centuries before it, the gateway to the castle precincts lay on the south side, well outside the town. The grammar school, likewise, has been moved to a far larger site on the right bank of the Eden, but its late Georgian building—replacing those where George Washington's father and half-brothers were educated—still stands in the present Chapel Street, and the stones that Bainbridge carved with antique inscriptions, and an original one of his own, are built into the roadside wall.

Despite its position, the actual town of Appleby was not part of the Clifford inheritance. In the 12th century all this property had belonged to the de Morville family. After Hugh de Morville had taken part in the murder of archbishop Thomas Becket in his own cathedral of Canterbury, and the subsequent rebellion of the 'young king Henry' against his father Henry II, the de Morville estates were forfeited to the Crown, and in 1174 Appleby and its castle were occupied by the invading Scots, who made it their headquarters for a time, but wasted the countryside on withdrawing after their defeat at Alnwick. King Henry looked on this repulse as an answer to his act of penance at the saint's shrine. He went as far as the midlands to assess and, as far as possible, to repair the damage, and it would seem to be then that he gave his town of Appleby its charter as an independent borough. The original charter of incorporation is lost, but a still-extant document of 1179, with the remains of the King's Great Seal, confirmed the borough in its rights and privileges when the castle was granted to another vassal, and it was duly accepted in later years as having a charter 'by prescription', even though it could no longer produce that first document of all. It was one of the oldest boroughs in England, and among the very first to have a mayor, and it is recorded that as late as the 19th century that official 'by immemorial custom' took precedence even of the Judge of Assize, the visiting embodiment of the King's Justice having to give place to the resident representative of the King himself. It was

Henry II who had established and organised the assize
system all over the country in 1176, so this exception
to the general practice may well have been deliberate, a
privilege granted to his already-existing royal borough
of Appleby.

King John confirmed his father's charter in 1200, and
three years later he granted to Robert de Vipont and
Idonea his wife 'Appleby and Brough', with the sheriff-
wick and rent of the county of Westmorland. By virtue
of the earlier charter of independence, the 'Appleby' of
this grant denoted only the castle and the ward of
Bongate across the river, and this, and not the town,
was what passed, in course of time, to the Cliffords
and their descendants. The point is an important one,
as it will be found to elucidate a reference in Lady
Anne's diary at the time of her mother's funeral.

Roger de Clifford and Roger de Leybourne, husbands
of Robert de Vipont's two daughters, tried to exercise
authority over Appleby as well, but in 1275 the burgesses
brought a writ against them, declaring themselves to be
tenants of the Crown and not of the Viponts or their
heirs, and the case was decided in their favour. A borough
that had no coat-of-arms of its own would customarily
display that of its feudal overlord, so the 13th-century
seal and counterseal of Appleby, still preserved among
the borough insignia, display neither the annulets of
Vipont nor the fess and chequers of Clifford, but the
three leopards that were the royal arms of England.
In later years, when this point had been forgotten, it
was assumed that the arms were those of the borough, and
to distinguish them from those of the sovereign the
leopards were arbitrarily described as crowned. The seal
was cited, in the 17th and 18th centuries, as authority
for this ingenious amendment, but it was quite unjustifi-
able, and in point of fact the seal and counterseal, with
their uncrowned leopards of England, still exist to give
it the lie.

This visit of Lady Cumberland and her daughter is
recorded in later years as 'the first tyme the La. Ann

Clifford cam into Westmd. or so far Northward', and there is no detailed mention of their residence in Appleby Castle. We know rather more about Brougham, where the dowager Countess lived for the greater part of her widowhood, dying in the room in which her husband had been born nearly 60 years before. Lady Anne came to live in it in her turn, in later life, and mentions that it communicated directly with a passage-room on the east side, and also with the central room of the keep. This establishes it as the second-floor room in the inner gatehouse, which stands immediately adjoining the Norman keep, not separated from it as at Appleby and Brough, but attributed, like them, to the Romans by popular tradition in Lady Anne's day. At Brougham the keep was known as the Pagan Tower, at Appleby it was Caesar's Tower—a name that it still bears in familiar speech—and at Brough, plainly and simply, the Roman Tower. Brough and Brougham are both on the sites of Roman forts, and the recent discovery of a Roman well under the castle at Appleby suggests the presence of a Roman guard-post overlooking the ford of the Eden before ever the town and its bridge were built, so that the ascription may owe something to a tenuous folk-memory as well as to a conventional legend. In these names, as in Camden's archaeological account of the region, we find the notion of a countryside of barren moorland and thin pasture, dominated here and there by ruined or half-ruined towers dating back, in popular imagination, to 'the most high and palmy state of Rome', a picture of past grandeur declining into desolation. To the widow and orphan of Clifford of Cumberland it may well have seemed a fit setting for their present disinherited state.

But the dowager countess was not one to waste time in unprofitable despair. Already, in her married life, she had had much to bear, and had borne it with uncomplaining patience; now, as time went on, she was to show herself not only patient but indomitable. That visit to the north played its part in a long, quiet determined and ultimately successful investigation into

the historical and legal background of the Clifford
inheritance, and established, as early as possible, a personal
contact with the Westmorland estates. They were hers for
her lifetime, she contemplated living there when her
daughter should be married and have a household of her
own, and it was good policy to pay an early visit and
make herself known to her tenants and neighbours.

Even before this, investigations had been set on foot
about another matter, which her husband had apparently
overlooked. Though the earldom of Cumberland was
restricted to the male line of descent, the baronies of
Clifford, Westmorland and Vescy were not, and should
have passed by right to his daughter Anne. In the first
months of her widowhood the countess employed one
St. Lo Kynaston to collect the detailed evidence in
support of this contention, and his researches amassed
in due course a formidable array of traditions, precedents,
modern instances and legal decisions regarding inheritance
through the female line. In her daughter's own words,
'she shewed herself so wise and industrious that she caused
diligent search to be made amongst the records of this
kingdom touching those ancient lands, and caused copies
to be taken out of them of such records as concerned
her said daughter's inheritance', and that wisdom and
industry were being exercised with a provident eye to
the future. While she lived, the 'ancient lands' were
indubitably hers, but she would not always live. Sooner
or later there would come a time when they must pass
to another, and under the terms of her husband's will
the inheritor would be his brother, not the daughter
to whom they ought, by right and precedent, to descend.
If there were anything to be done that might ensure this,
or at least show cause for such a course, then the sooner
it were done, or at least prepared, the better for the
claimant.

Meanwhile, even without this uncertain possibility,
the young Lady Anne was in her own right a considerable
heiress, and took part in the fashionable entertainments
of the Court. At 17 she danced in Ben Jonson's *Masque*

of Beauty, as one of the Queen's attendant ladies, and two years later, in his *Masque of Queens*, she danced again, as Berenice of Egypt, in a costume designed for her by Inigo Jones. There may well have been a particular compliment intended in casting her for the part, since Berenice was famous for the beauty of her hair—there is an allusion to it in Jonson's text—and Lady Anne recalled in later years that when she was young her hair was long enough to hang down to her calves when she stood upright. The head-dress of the masquing costume does not allow for any such display, but this is to be expected, since Berenice was known to have sacrificed her beautiful hair as a votive offering for the safe return of her husband Ptolemy Euergetes from a campaign.

In this same month, February 1609, Lady Anne married. Her husband was Richard Sackville, very soon to become Earl of Dorset. He had begun his courtship some two years before, as his grandfather had written in April 1607 to Sir George Moore stating his own desire for the match, and asking Sir George to use his good offices with the dowager Lady Cumberland to bring it about. Indeed, this may be the very alliance to which Lady Anne had referred as far back as 1605, when she wrote to her mother about 'that matter you know of, for that match', which her father had been discussing with her at such length a few months before his death. Now the bridegroom's father in his turn lay on his deathbed, and a contemporary letter-writer, the shrewd and observant John Chamberlain, commented that the marriage had been hastened on, so that young Sackville might not be a bachelor when the time came to inherit the family titles and estates.

Had he been so, the plan might well have gone awry. He was still only 19, so he would have become a ward of the Court, and his marriage would be arranged by whatever guardian the King, or the Court of Wards and Liveries, thought fit to appoint for him. (Chamberlain names the Earl of Lennox as having aspirations in that

direction.) The system of wardship had originated in the
days when a feudal overlord had the responsibility of
protecting the widows and orphans of his tenants against
rapacious neighbours, but by the 17th century it had been
abandoned in most European countries and, though still
in force in England, was being increasingly criticised as
an undesirable anachronism. Under the presidency of a
conscientious official like the great Lord Burghley, the
Court of Wards had still carried out its functions honour-
ably and efficiently, as well Lady Cumberland knew,
since her own husband had been brought up in boyhood
as her father's ward, but even then the system itself
had been shown to have its drawbacks. Now, with a
different sovereign on the throne and very different
characters about him, its unsatisfactory qualities were
being made manifest. Shakespeare, in *All's Well that
Ends Well,* had shown what trouble and hard feeling
it could cause when operated even from the best of
motives, and there was no denying that unscrupulous
people could, and on occasion did, petition (and pay)
to be appointed guardians to heirs and heiresses purely
as an investment, with a view to arranging marriages
for them in due course at considerable profit to
themselves.

This was just what might have happened to Lady
Anne on her father's death, had she not successfully
petitioned at once to have her mother appointed her
legal guardian. That appointment entitled the dowager
Lady Cumberland to start and carry on her campaign,
on her daughter's behalf, for the Clifford property in
Craven, and for the succession to the Westmorland
estates that had formed her own jointure. With her
experience and foresight she would appreciate and approve
this early marriage of two minors, and indeed she may
well have suggested it, since we know from Lady Anne's
own notes that it was celebrated 'in my mother's house,
and her own Chamber, in Augustine Fryers in London,
which was part of a Chapel there formerly', and that
Lady Cumberland herself was present. It looks very much

as if the dowager had seen what was coming, and had taken prudent and speedy action to safeguard the position of young Lord Buckhurst, as he then was. He succeeded to his earldom only two days later, but by that time he was no longer a potential source of profit to speculators in the marriage-market, for he was himself a married man. Lady Anne likewise, though officially safe under her mother's guardianship, had been spoken of in Court circles and Chamberlain's correspondence as a likely bride for the King's favourite, Robert Carr, soon to become the notorious Earl of Somerset. In the light of what happened afterwards, it is clear that some pressure might have been put upon mother and daughter to compel them to agree to this most undesirable match, so it was good policy to arrange and perform a more satisfactory marriage with the least possible delay.

Like almost any other desirable end, it was achieved at a price. The safe transference of the heiress into the guardianship of a husband meant the breaking of the long association that had existed between her and her mother for so many years. Lady Cumberland's estrangement from her husband had concentrated her affection all the more strongly on her only surviving child, and the two had been conscious allies ever since little Anne's babyhood. Now the time had come for a great change in the lives of both. The new Lady Dorset must go down into Kent to assume her duties as mistress of the great house of Knole, and her mother, lonely as she had never been before, must turn her face to the north and settle down in the old crumbling castle beside the Eamont, where she was still little more than a newcomer, some three hundred miles away. The estates that waited for her there were very different from the Northamptonshire countryside where she had spent much of her childhood, wilder even than the lands of Skipton-in-Craven, where she had been brought as a bride. Brougham she had known only from occasional visits with her husband, who had been born there, but now she was to live there all the year round, and to be in responsible control of her numerous tenants, herself dwelling in one of those masses of masonry that were looked upon as monuments of forgotten greatness. Shakespeare, coming from the kindly countryside of Warwickshire and writing for an audience of Londoners, well expresses the general feeling when he refers to a castle in Northumberland, in the prologue to the *Second Part of King Henry IV,* as 'this worm-eaten hold of ragged stone'. It was to just such a 'hold', among the wild waste lands under the fells, that the dowager was to withdraw for the rest of her days.

Chapter Three

THE CHANGING AGE

When the son dies, let the inheritance
Descend unto the daughter
Henry V, I, ii

THE NEW LADY DORSET was very happy in the first
months of her marriage. Her husband was popular,
affectionate, well-read and 'in his owne Nature of a just
mynde, of a sweete Disposition, and verie valiant in his
owne person', besides being generous to the point of
prodigality, especially to scholars and soldiers and indeed
'any of worth that were in distress', to a greater degree
than he could really afford. Lady Anne's choice of
words here is quite significant. The combination of scholar
and soldier made up the ideal Elizabethan gentleman—a
man like 'the miracle of our age, Sir Philip Sidney', as
Carew puts it in his contribution to Camden's *Remaines.*
Nerissa calls Bassanio 'a scholar and a soldier' when
praising him to her mistress in the second scene of *The
Merchant of Venice,* and Hamlet appeals to his companions
on their honour as 'friends, scholars and soldiers' when
swearing them to secrecy after his interview with his
father's ghost, while a few years later Shakespeare is
found bracketing a third quality with the former two
and using the blend of soldier, statesman and scholar as
a term of highest praise in *Measure for Measure.*

All the same, there was a change coming, and in the
new generation it was very noticeable. Lady Anne's
father had been a man of action, and his lavish expenditure
had been devoted to the furthering of his adventurous
expeditions abroad. Her husband was a great spender
likewise, but his money went not on doing such things
himself but on encouraging and rewarding other men
who did them, leaving him free thereby to pursue his
own pleasures. The change is mirrored in Shakespeare

once again, when we see his portrayal of Timon of Athens, a man essentially noble by nature, generous to scholars, artists and the soldier Alcibiades, but lacking alike the intellectual training to foresee and avoid disaster and the mental discipline to endure it when it comes upon him. It is a striking and compassionate study of a tendency observed and far more mercilessly castigated by Jonson in characters like Volpone and Sir Epicure Mammon.

It was, after all, the tendency of the age, and in a time of general peace and prosperity there is a strong temptation to admire, encourage and patronise these and other virtues as a pleasant alternative to practising them. Young Dorset was doing what most other young men of good family thought fit to do, and for a little while, at least, he had enough money to do it. The sports of the tilt-yard, in which he excelled, were active still, but with a different activity from that of an earlier day. Men still contested with each other, to the admiration of the spectators, but more often in rivalry than in direct opposition. A man showed his horsemanship by riding in a race, or in something like modern show-jumping, and his skill with the lance was demonstrated by riding at a suspended ring, not at a similarly-armed adversary who was equally keen to strike him on helmet or breastplate, and perhaps knock him out of the saddle. The specially-reinforced armour of the former generation was no longer generally required, for the emphasis in these contests was laid on elegance and accuracy, not on endurance, and the competitors aimed their lances at a piece of apparatus that had no power of hitting back. When Dorset had his portrait painted in miniature by Isaac Oliver, he was shown wearing a suit of blue—a most unusual and unfashionable colour for persons of quality. Blue was the colour of the hard-wearing, indigo-dyed material used for the coats of serving-men, scholars at charitable institutions (as in the honoured traditional dress worn at Christ's Hospital) and soldiers of the rank and file. A nobleman might dress his servants in it, but would not normally be seen wearing it himself, unless he were being deliberately democratic or displaying soldierly pretensions. Dorset is shown standing by his armour as if he were ready to equip himself at any moment for the fashionable 'combat at barriers', where no leg-armour was required. Below the waist, therefore, he wears the soldier's colour, but a look at his doublet, his lace and the fashionable rosettes upon his shoes will make it clear at once that if he is indeed dressed for the Simple Life, he is dressed for it by a very expensive tailor.

One of his closest friends was young Prince Henry, the King's eldest son, who was created Prince of Wales in 1610. The accompanying festivities included *Tethys' Festival,* a masque written by the scholar and poet Samuel Daniel, who had been tutor to Lady Anne in her childhood. The part of Tethys herself was played by the Queen, while certain of her ladies represented the nymphs of the great rivers of England, each with some appropriateness to her origin or estate. Princess Elizabeth, the King's daughter, played the Thames, her north-country cousin, Arabella Stuart the Trent, the Countess of Montgomery the Severn, and young Lady Dorset the Aire, which flowed by the castle of Skipton, where she had been born. Other performers in the festivities included the young Countess of Essex, Dorset's first cousin, and the 'incomparable pair of brethren', William and Philip Herbert, Earls of Pembroke and Montgomery respectively, who appeared in the tilt-yard on the third day. All these three were to achieve notoriety of different kinds in the succeeding years, the two brothers as patrons of literature and art—the famous First Folio of Shakespeare's plays was dedicated to them—and the Countess as arranging a particularly scandalous and discreditable divorce from her husband, and instigating the murder of her lover's friend, Sir Thomas Overbury, who knew rather too much about her for her peace of mind. But in 1610 these vicissitudes were all reasonably far ahead, and they danced and made merry and were young.

Next year there was a minor sensation, which might have developed into a scandal if prompt action had not suppressed it. A young Oxford theologian called Anthony Stafford brought out the first of a series of publications that were ultimately to earn him a certain amount of notoriety and, in Puritan quarters, disapproval, as savouring too strongly of Roman Catholicism in general and the cult of the Virgin Mary in particular. It was called *Stafford's Niobe*, and came out in two parts, the first being dedicated, quite unexceptionally, to Robert Cecil, Earl of Salisbury. The second volume, however, comes as something of a surprise in this respect. Its dedication is addressed, not to an elderly and important public figure, but to the young Countess of Dorset, and is worded throughout in terms of amazed and respectful admiration. The impression given is that the writer has been suddenly, completely and unalterably captivated by the lady's incomparable qualities of mind and body, and has been compelled, however reluctantly, to revise his hitherto unflattering opinion of her whole sex. It is the kind of thing that might well have been addressed, ten years earlier, to the elderly Elizabeth—who would have considered it a very proper style for the author to adopt, without for one moment believing that he meant it—but to single out in such a way a young, recently-married noblewoman was very different and by no means admirable. The Court of James and Anne was not what it had been in the days of Elizabeth, and for anyone who achieved notoriety there was a real risk of being credited with the worst possible reasons for it. Plenty of people, in the Court and out of it, would be ready to say 'Praise to the face is open disgrace', and that in its turn would lead others to say that there was no smoke without fire, if something were not done at once to put a stop to it.

But quite obviously something *was* done, and done so promptly and efficiently that the indiscreet publication was suppressed before ever it could reach the eye of the general reader. Investigations by Dr. Williamson, in or about 1920, showed that almost every known copy of the book bore no trace at all of this dedication, the offending pages having been removed before binding. In one copy, on the market at the time of the investigation, the main text of the dedication was present, but the first page had been torn out, so that there was no indication of the name of the lady so embarrassingly addressed. The copy in the Bodleian Library had also lost the greater part of its first page, but here by chance (or is it by design?) the remaining fragment contains Lady Anne's name after all. From the British Museum copy, and from all the others save one, the dedication-pages appear to have been deliberately omitted. One solitary copy, in the Huth Library, contains the dedication in full, and must have escaped the general purge.

We have no direct record to tell us how that rapid piece of censorship was carried out, but one or two points are perhaps worth considering in this respect. Lord Dorset and Anthony Stafford were of an age to have been near-contemporaries at Oxford, Dorset being the younger by two years. When he was an undergraduate, his grandfather was chancellor of the university, and was known to take his duties seriously and interest himself in the work that was being done there. The grandson in his turn had learnt early in life to look with appreciation on the labours of the professional scholar, and was just the sort of person whose interest and perhaps friendship would be of the greatest encouragement to a writer like Stafford. Accordingly, when that pious and scholarly young man published his first book, and it succeeded, it might well seem to him that the sequel would give him a chance to make his acknowledgments to his young friend by paying a compliment to that friend's young and charming wife. Unfortunately, he overdid it, and his good intentions went very wrong indeed, but it looks as if the *faux pas* had been observed, and deplored, on sight of the first advance copies, before the bulk of the edition had been bound for general issue. Personal remonstration with the author, and hurried, conscience-stricken orders from him to the printer, would reasonably account for the rapid and unobtrusive removal of the dedication before the book appeared on the market, and all was well. Discretion, promptitude and common-sense had settled the affair in the best possible way before the Court gossips could get to hear of it. Dorset was free to travel abroad for the best part of a year, and his lady went down into Kent to occupy herself with the house affairs at Knole.

That matter was happily concluded, but there was another in which, from the very first, the young husband and wife did not see eye to eye, and as time went on it was to cause great unhappiness between them. Dorset had no feeling for those far-off lands in the north, by which his wife and her mother set such great store, nor for the estates in Craven now enjoyed by her uncle Cumberland. His heart and his interests were in the surroundings of the Court and the social and sporting events of fashionable life. Knole in Kent and Bolebrook in Sussex could give him all he needed in the way of country recreation, and were not only comfortable in themselves, but lay in easy reach of Whitehall and all that went on there. He had no sympathy, and would pretend none, for his wife's determination to hold on, at all costs, to the inheritance of her forefathers. To him, that region of barren moors and ruinous, legendary towers was an alien land, and to live there, as Lady Cumberland was doing, would be little better than exile.

It was not the same, naturally, for everyone. His wife's uncle, who had inherited the earldom, was not so essentially bound to the interests and amusements of the Court. Rightly or wrongly, he and his son had got possession of the Yorkshire lands, and there was every likelihood of their obtaining the Westmorland estates as well, when the dowager should die. They had got most of the property, and he had not; they wanted the rest of it, and he did not. What his wife wanted need not be considered. Insistence on her claim only meant stirring up trouble in unsuitable quarters, as the King himself was inclined to favour the present state of things. From his point of view, an amicable settlement or 'composition' would be much the best thing for all concerned. Cumberland would be left in possession of the property he already held, and the reversion of the rest in some years' time, but he would not be so unreasonable as to expect all this for nothing, and quite obviously he could afford to pay for it. For the kind of life that Dorset lived, and enjoyed, and intended to go on living and enjoying, money was essential, and a cash 'composition' at home was infinitely preferable to a barren lordship in the north—if only his wife could be persuaded to see reason and look at the matter in the same way. She remained, however, resolute in her conviction that her claim was not an affair of compromise or arrangement, but of simple right, and he was not pleased.

Other things occurred at this time to trouble her. In the year of her husband's return from abroad she lost a dearly-loved cousin, Lady Frances Bourchier, daughter of her mother's sister, the Countess of Bath. Their affection dated from the spring of 1603, when the two countesses had suits to pursue at the Court of the new King and Queen, and their daughters were continually in each other's company. Lady Frances was then 17, and might have thought herself too old for the 13-year-old Anne, but the child was a daily visitor at Bath House and, in her own words, 'grew daily more inward with my cousin *Frances* and Mrs *Carey*', the latter of whom was beginning to interest a couple of young Scottish noblemen about the Court. When they went on a visit to another aunt, the Countess of Warwick, little Anne was severely scolded by her mother for riding on ahead with one of the gentlemen in attendance. There was an epidemic of plague in the neighbourhood, and he probably showed signs of illness—indeed, he collapsed and died next day—so that there would be an instant fear of infection. Partly for that reason, and partly as a punishment for her indiscretion, Anne was isolated by being locked in a bedroom by herself for the night, but, as she later recorded, 'my cousin *Frances* got the key of my chamber and lay with me which was the first time I loved her so well'.

That piece of surreptitious kindness and understanding, from one who was almost grown-up, meant a great deal to the unhappy little girl, and quite obviously she never forgot it. Now, with her mother away in the north, her father's kinfolk—and, it would seem, her husband himself —ranged against her in the dispute over her inheritance, she was very much alone. She might be expected to turn to the friend who had come, years before, to comfort her in her loneliness, but even that relief was denied her. At her aunt Cumberland's house of Sutton in Kent, not so far from Knole, Lady Frances died 'of a burning fever' at the age of 22, and Lady Anne ordered a monument of black and white marble to be set up for her in the church at Chenies in Buckinghamshire, where she is buried.

Two other losses, one personal and the other national, were to fall upon her before the end of the year. One was that of the dowager Lady Bedford, her mother's stepmother, who had a sudden stroke and did not recover. At the beginning of the reign she had been one of the greatest ladies in the land, and ranked highest in the favour of the Queen, whom she had attended on her first journey out of Scotland into her husband's new kingdom. Her passing meant the breaking of yet another link with the old days and the now almost legendary Court of Elizabeth, and it is not surprising that Dorset, in a letter, mentions that his wife is unable to write because 'she is so full of sorrow and so unfit'.

With that figure from the past had gone, independently, the country's main hope for the future. Only a few days before, men had been shocked by the news of the death of Henry, Prince of Wales, at the age of eighteen. The sense of loss was widespread, as the young prince had been regarded as the embodiment of practically all that Englishmen wanted to see in their future King. Rightly or wrongly, he was credited with his father's intelligence without his physical ungainliness, and his mother's good-fellowship without her triviality and frivolity. In him men saw, or hoped to see, that ideal combination of scholar, sportsman, statesman, and, if necessary, soldier, that implied a return to the golden age of 100 years before, when the Court was full of money and Henry VIII was young.

Now, all these hopes were suddenly at an end. His death, thought to have been from typhoid fever, was widely and resentfully ascribed to poison. His body was buried in state at Westminster, in the same vault as his grandmother, Mary Queen of Scots; his splendid armour—the last really fine suit to be produced by the Greenwich workshops—was laid aside, to be exhibited later in the century on a portrait-statue of him in the Tower, and in another part of that same Tower the ageing Ralegh, last of the great Elizabethans, brought to a close the first volume of his vast *History of the World* with a short, sad paragraph announcing that the rest of the work would never be written. Prince Henry's interest and enthusiasm had encouraged him to conceive and begin the enterprise, and it had occupied years of his time while he lay a prisoner under a sentence of death that had been suspended but never repealed and was in fact to be put into execution some years later still. His object had been to 'lay before the eyes of the living the fall and fortunes of the dead' for the guidance and edification of a future King of England, and he had perservered in spite of many discouragements, but with the death of his young patron the whole work came to an abrupt end when it had got no further than the heyday of republican Rome. The shock and sadness of the author are still conveyed, in some degree, to the reader of the last pages. Without warning, the narrative gives place to a summary of the whole matter in the conclusion that 'the Kings and Princes of the world have alwayes laid before them, the actions, but not the ends of those great Ones which praeceded them . . . They neglect the advice of GOD, while they enjoy life, or hope it; but they follow the counsell of Death, upon his first approach'. The grave and noble panegyric upon death, which follows, is probably the best-known part of the whole work, and after it comes the brief, sad statement that though a second and third volume had been originally intended, 'besides many other discouragements, perswading my silence; it hath pleased GOD to take that glorious *Prince* out of the world, to whom they were directed', so that there was no longer any point in going on. The young man's friendship and encouragement had been Ralegh's last hope, and now he had nothing to hope for, or to look forward to, any more.

Dorset himself, in very different circumstances, felt much the same. His wife more than once pays tribute to his kindly and affectionate nature, and there is no reason to doubt his sincerity when he says, in his own correspondence, how much he felt the loss. The prince and he had been close companions in many sporting and social activities, making their appearance armed in the tilt-yard or gorgeously and fantastically attired in some splendid festivity at Whitehall. The loss meant the breaking up of a pattern, like the shaking of a kaleidoscope, and the remaining pieces would have to rearrange themselves as best they might.

They did so, and in ways that meant strain and unhappiness for Lady Anne. The Court, as soon as its official mourning was over, threw itself energetically into the arrangements for the marriage of Elizabeth, the dead prince's sister, to the Elector Palatine. Dorset's reaction was characteristic. He made himself conspicuous for splendour, activity and extravagance, aroused practically universal admiration, and spent a great deal of money which by this time he could ill afford. The wedding was celebrated in February 1613, and it has been plausibly conjectured that Shakespeare wrote *The Tempest* for performance in the course of the festivities.

It is to this period that we may ascribe the introduction of another figure who was to cause Lady Anne much unhappiness in the succeeding years. On a list at Knole, enumerating all the household, occurs the name of

Mr. Matthew Caldicott, enigmatically described as 'my Lord's favourite', dining at the parlour table with the chaplain, the steward and other senior officials, while 'my lord's table' was reserved for the family. What with his friend's death and the breaking-up of what had been a lively and entertaining Court circle, Dorset must have felt lost without an object for his immediate affections. He was not yet 25, and would feel the need for someone who could be at once a companion, a confidant and, when necessary, a sympathetic audience. Passionate and emotional attachments between young men were not uncommon at Whitehall and around it in the days of King James, and a man in Dorset's position would badly need someone to whom he could lament his loss and complain about his wife.

For, in his view, there was grave cause for complaint. The life he was leading in general, and the part he was playing in the entertainments that accompanied the royal wedding, cost a great deal of money, and money was running short. His lady was an heiress, it was true, but her heritage was largely tied up in landed estates and too far off, in time and place, to be of any use to him in his immediate needs. Her father's property in Craven, and probably the reversion of her mother's jointure lands in Westmorland, had been left to her uncle. She had the ultimate reversion in default of his leaving male heirs, but in the meantime he might—and, in fact, did—live for years. And in any case, the ownership of large but comparatively barren estates far away in the midlands and further north still, almost on the Border, was of little use to a nobleman who was a popular and extravagant figure in fashionable life and meant to stay so. He would much rather have cash, and the exasperating thing was that he had a reasonable chance of getting it, if only Lady Anne could be persuaded to see the matter from his point of view. Her uncle Cumberland had no intention of surrendering the estates his brother had bequeathed to him, but he was prepared to come to an arrangement and make an *ex gratia* payment to his niece, partly to avoid a tiresome and acrimonious family law-suit and partly, perhaps, out of a genuine feeling of sympathy for her in her disappointment. A money settlement would allow him undisturbed possession of the property, so that he could continue as the country landowner that he was, and liked to be, while she—or at any rate her husband—would find it far more satisfactory to have cash in hand for the maintenance of their own very different way of life. It was not in accordance with the strict letter of the law, but it seemed to him, and to a good many other people, a very sensible and not ungenerous compromise.

It did not seem so, however, to Lady Anne, who was as resolute as Naboth not to surrender the inheritance of her father. She was ready to pay tribute to the kindness and affection of her husband, and she described her uncle as 'an honourable gentleman, and of a good, noble, sweet and courteous nature', but that did not mean that she would say what they did was right when she was convinced, by the legal evidence and her own conscience, that it was wrong. By way of making allowances for them both, she was ready to believe that they were urged on by others, her uncle by his son, who in her words 'did absolutely govern' both him and his estates, and Dorset by his brother Edward, whom she disliked and distrusted, and who eventually succeeded him in the earldom. Husband and wife were on close and affectionate terms in all matters but this, and at Great Dorset House in July 1614, their first child was born, a daughter. The dowager Lady Cumberland had come down from Brougham for the occasion, but missed being present at the birth, having gone to the Tower 'about business'—possibly connected with evidence about the rights of the Cliffords, since the public records were kept in the Tower at the time—and failed to leave it before the gates of the fortress were shut for the night. At the christening she stood godmother to the child, who was named Margaret after her, and in less than a week she took leave of her grandchild and her son-in-law for the last time, when the household moved down to Knole. A few days later she left her own house in Austin Friars and set off on her journey back to Brougham, never to return.

Her daughter's letters to her in the succeeding months have been preserved, and give an expressive account of the progress of their affairs, and characteristic news about the baby, sometimes looking very smart in the 'delicate fine little gloves' sent by her grandmother, and now and then 'very froward' with the trouble of teething. Lord Dorset is obdurate about the Westmorland inheritance, but kind and characteristically generous in other matters. For instance, he has agreed to redeem for a hundred pounds (though he has to borrow the money himself) a chain which Lady Cumberland has pledged to a London goldsmith, if she will let him know the man's name and the sign of his shop, and Lady Anne will arrange for the chain to be sold in order to pay the money back. At the same time, she is on the look-out to see if there is any sign of his concluding an independent arrangement with her uncle, and if so, she will let her mother know at once. Her suit about the inheritance is still dragging on in the courts, and though in one letter she confidently hopes to visit Westmorland herself before the end of the summer, a letter in June gives the bad news that 'my Lord will not by any means give his consent that I should go, till the business between my uncle of Cumberland and him be ended'. She respectfully begs her mother to be on better terms with Lord William Howard, assuring her that he was 'very forward in my business', but the later course of events indicates that the older woman had summed him up better than her daughter, and was quite right in her opinion.

In November 1615 she touches, with considerable discretion, on a famous Jacobean scandal. 'For the news of the town and wonder of the world, this business of my Lord of Somerset and his Lady, I will forbear to write and leave them to the relation of this honest bearer, Mr Clapham, for my eyes are still very sore'.

The Lord Somerset whom she mentions was that Robert Carr, once rumoured as a possible husband for herself, and his lady was her husband's cousin Frances Howard, who had obtained a divorce from her first husband, the second Earl of Essex (on grounds which a good many people disbelieved in) and married Carr. The King shortly afterwards raised him to the earldom of Somerset, but the whole affair aroused a great deal of talk and some disapproval. One person who had been firmly against the marriage, and the intrigue that had preceded it, had been Carr's friend, Sir Thomas Overbury, who had considerable influence over him. This displeased the King, who tried to have Overbury posted abroad, and when he declined to go, sent him to the Tower for disobedience. Presently he died there of an unexplained illness, and the way was clear for Carr to proceed with the wedding. In the succeeding months came the rumour that Overbury's death had not been a natural one, and it was decided, in due course, that he had been poisoned, and that various members of the Howard family were concerned in it. The Lieutenant of the Tower, Sir Gervase Helwys, had been recently appointed to his post by the influence of Lady Somerset's father, who was Lord Chamberlain at the time; he was found to have been in correspondence with her great-uncle, the Earl of Northampton, who was Lord Privy Seal, and he himself, if not guilty, must have been singularly ignorant and criminally negligent. All things considered, there would be a great deal, by this time, that Lady Anne found it better to send by word of mouth than to write down, but a postscript to her next letter, ten days later, announced that Helwys had been hanged that day at Tower Hill for complicity in the murder.

Dorset's mother had been a Howard, the sister of Lady Somerset's father, so that in addition to his financial difficulties he had a good deal on his mind. Again and again, however, Lady Anne insists, in her letters and diaries, on his kindness and affection for her and for their child, and his continued consideration for her in all matters except that of the inheritance, which appears to change his nature completely and makes him a different man. He himself, in his correspondence, is revealed as feeling almost exactly the same about her. After all, their mutual understanding and affection went back to the days of their relative youth, and was too deeply seated to be easily done away with, but that very fact made it easier for them both, over this one point, to wound and torment each other and themselves.

Michaelmas law term had come to an end, a new year was beginning, and the case was still undecided. Lord Dorset was getting desperate for money, his lady was still obstinate in alliance with her mother, and it was obvious that he must put increasing pressure on her if he were to get the action settled. It is possible that she realised this as well as he, for there exists at Knole a copy of a diary covering the next few years, in which she has recorded in detail the progress of the affair. It is in a clerkly 18th-century hand, and bears not only notes and marginalia that were obviously written by the diarist, but other explanatory footnotes in a hand not yet identified. The original, in Lady Anne's writing, has not been traced, but the fair copy was edited and published in 1923 by Miss V. Sackville-West.

A brief autobiographical note tells of Lady Anne's childhood, Queen Elizabeth's death, with the accession and arrival of King James and his consort, and the regrettable fact that very soon the reputation of the Court sank considerably, so that 'it was grown a scandalous place', and not at all what it had been in the days of Elizabeth. From these generalities the manuscript makes a leap of some 12 years, to New Year's Day 1616, going on from there in regular diary form. It may be that Lady Anne was compiling either a record for her own perusal or, more probably, a memorandum for someone else's, since if it is considered as an account of the contest for the Westmorland estates, it at once becomes more coherent. The seemingly irrelevant opening falls

into place as a necessary preparation for the reader, giving
a brief but clear account of the relations between Lord and
Lady Cumberland, the arrival of a new sovereign and the
practically immediate alteration of Court life and Court
standards of behaviour. Lady Anne had obviously never
forgotten that unfortunate experience at Theobalds when
she and her mother went to pay their respects to the
new King. With this brief prologue the characters are
introduced, their background indicated and some explanation given of Lady Anne's principles, and the
grounds for them.

The year begins quietly enough. On New Year's Day
Lord Dorset and all the house-party went to see the
New Year Masque at Court. His lady stayed in her room
all day—possibly she had not been well—but a few days
later she was able to see the masque from Lady Arundel's
box when the performance was repeated on Twelfth
Night, and two days after that, on the 8th, she notes
that she went to see Lady Ralegh at the Tower, where
Sir Walter was undergoing the final months of his long
imprisonment, before that last fruitless voyage to Guiana
that was to destroy his hopes, his son and, on his return,
his very life. In a letter written on the 20th, she tells
her mother, with some pleasure, of the release of Lady
Shrewsbury from the Tower. This was the mother of that
Lady Arundel with whom she had supped and gone to
the masque a fortnight before, and the party may have
been in some degree a celebration, but it is clear that
her own position, in regard to the inheritance, was
rapidly becoming desperate. She was being pressed to
renounce her claim to her mother's jointure land, and
threatened with the severest penalty that her husband
could inflict on her—the break-up of their marriage. If
he were unable to settle some, at least, of his debts,
and to go on living in the style that he preferred, he
might very well have to leave the country and live, an
insolvent exile, in France, and she would be to blame
for it. To some people, at any rate, her duty to her
husband was clearly to comply, but there were certain

considerations to be put into the other scale, and these would do much to even the balance.

First, in her mind, came the duty and affection she owed to her mother. Ever since her widowhood, more than 10 years before, Lady Cumberland had worked to ensure the settlement of Appleby and Brougham, and their accompanying castles and lands at Brough and Pendragon, upon her daughter. She had done much, and spent much, and put up with much, to find every scrap of evidence, every argument of law and equity, and bring them to the notice of those most likely to establish her in her claim. To that daughter it was unthinkable that she should go behind her mother's back, and make all that work and endurance fruitless by an act of independent capitulation. In the second place, there was the feeling of another betrayal. To surrender her rights in the way her husband wished would mean not only that she could not claim those lands on her mother's death, but that she would never get them at all. Her father's will, wrong-headed as she thought it, had at least reserved to her the ultimate reversion if her uncle and cousin should die without male heirs. It had been perhaps a weak attempt to bring back the property, in an unlikely contingency, to the line in which it had been established, and showed some faint and dubious consideration for his own daughter. Now she was being asked to surrender even that.

And, underlying everything, we must imagine the core of hard, practical common-sense that was so characteristic of her in later years. There was no suggestion that this capitulation, and the ready money that it would bring, were needed to save her husband from immediate ruin and set him on his feet again with a view to living in a more modest style thereafter. He was living beyond his means, and intended to go on doing so. This sacrifice that meant so much to her would only postpone the catastrophe, not avert it. There were many well-meaning people, in the family and out of it, who were ready to lecture her on her duty as a wife, but it would not do any good to answer them that it was not her duty to throw good money after bad. The course they pressed upon her was not only repugnant to her sense of loyalty to her parents and her family tradition; much as she loved her husband she knew that it would not do him any good. This money would go, as the rest had gone, and after that there would be nothing.

Chapter Four

MOTHER AND DAUGHTER

Unkindness may do much;
And his unkindness may defeat my life,
But never taint my love.

Othello, IV, ii

AFTER THE FIRST few weeks of 1616, the real pressure began. It is perhaps significant that about this time Lady Anne went to Chenies, the home of her mother's sister, Lady Bath, to see the memorial that she had caused to be set up there for her beloved cousin Frances Bourchier, who had come by night to comfort her when she was frightened and alone so many years before. Now there was no hope of that; her mother was hundreds of miles away; her dear, understanding kinswoman was represented only by a monument and a memory, and she was indeed alone.

Life in the country was by no means all misery, however. In the Knole manuscript she admits that she was 'sometimes merry and sometimes sad', but a summons to London usually meant trouble. Early in February Lord Dorset sent for his wife to come up to London about the arrangement with her uncle and cousin. She notes that on the 12th, Lord Roos, son of the Earl of Exeter, was married to the daughter of Sir Thomas Lake, Secretary of State, but does not say in so many words that she and her husband were at the wedding. The fact may have been noted merely because Lake had been an adherent of their Howard relations, but it led to a notorious and unsavoury scandal later on. What was more important was that on the 15th Lady Grantham and Sir George Manners came to supper, and on the next day Lady Grantham urged her very earnestly to agree to the 'composition' with her cousins, saying that the Archbishop of Canterbury was arranging to visit her on the following day to talk about the matter.

Lady Anne took this warning as 'a great argument of her love', but it was rather a strain to be lectured severely by her 'cousin Russell' on the same day about the error of her ways. He left her in floods of tears, and she steadied herself by repeating a prayer and setting out on a social visit. She called on Lady Wotton, her first cousin, at Whitehall, and walked with her 'some five or six turns'. Neither of them mentioned the matter, though they were both thinking of it, and Lady Anne went on from there to a sight-seeing tour of the royal tombs in Westminster Abbey. King James had had the body of his mother, Mary Queen of Scots, brought from her grave in Peterborough Cathedral to lie at Westminster under a new and splendid monument, and it was naturally one of the latest sights of fashionable London. Lady Anne was interested in monumental architecture; it was not long since she had stood before her cousin's tomb at Chenies, and in a short time, though as yet she did not know it, she would be commissioning another in the north. She specifically mentions that she saw 'the Queen of *Scots,* her tomb and all the other tombs'— including, no doubt, the stern old effigy of Elizabeth, by whom she had been 'much beloved' as a little girl— and then came home by water from Westminster to Dorset House. In many ways the surface of the Thames was the pleasantest, easiest and quickest thoroughfare between Westminster and London, but it was not warm on a February afternoon. Lady Anne had had an emotional and exhausting day, her 'five or six turns' with Lady Wotton had been followed by a slower promenade from chapel to chapel on the hard pavements of the Abbey, and she must have been physically exhausted by the time she settled down upon the boat-cushions. There is always a chill wind upon the river, and what with unhappiness, physical weariness and apprehension of the morrow's interview, she can have had little power of resistance. In her own words, she 'took an extreme cold', and must have felt in very poor condition for her ordeal next day.

It was a solemn and oppressive affair indeed, held in the Gallery at Dorset House, and attended by 'a great company of men', all ranged implacably against her. There was her cousin Russell, who had given her such a scolding the day before, there was her husband's brother Edward, whom she disliked and distrusted, there was Lord William Howard, whom she trusted but her mother did not, there was the newly-married Lord Roos and a number of others whom the diary does not mention by name, and above all there was the Primate of All England, Archbishop Abbott himself. He took her aside for a private conference and lectured her for an hour and a half, urging her 'both by Divine and human means' to agree to the suggested compromise, but in spite of it all she remained obdurate. She would not sign anything, or agree to anything, without first discussing it with her mother. The family council in general took a hand, now with conciliation and now with warnings or threats, but among fears, tears and sneezes she held firmly to that one principle—that she would do nothing, and indeed *could* do nothing, independently of her mother, who had initiated the suit and was still living and entitled to her proper jointure lands. What must have exasperated the company was the fact that on this point, at any rate, she was unquestionably right. Frustrated and indignant, they finally agreed that she should go to Brougham as soon as possible, and that she and her mother should send an answer by the 22 March. The Archbishop and the other lords all signed a document to this effect, and poor Anne was free to nurse her cold and enjoy a short but blessed relief from her immediate anxiety. At one point it had seemed to her and to everyone that she must lose, on the spot, either her husband or her inheritance, but now she had a month's respite, and she was going to see her mother again. It was a marvellous deliverance, and in her memorandum of it she frankly said so.

There was no need for any delay. The great meeting had been held on the 17th of the month, and on the 19th two of Lady Anne's servants were going the round of her circle of acquaintances with the formal notice that she was leaving town. Next day there was a final visit from Lord Francis Russell—whom she noted as having been 'exceeding careful and kind' to her throughout the whole business, and whose lecture a few days earlier had clearly left no hard feelings—and on the 21st she and her husband actually set off for the north. Each of them had a coach with four horses, the escorting horsemen numbered 'about 26', and Lady Anne had two women in attendance, apparently Mrs. Willoughby, who sat at the top of the Parlour table at Knole, and Judith Simpton,* who had a similar position at the laundry-maids' table further down. Roads were primitive and ill-repaired, February was an ill month for travelling and progress was naturally slow. It took them nearly a week to get to Lichfield, and on the 26th, when they had got as far as Burton-on-Trent, Lord Dorset and his part of the company turned back, as he wanted to stay a few days in Lichfield for a race-meeting. For all we know, it may never have been intended that he should go right through to Brougham and take part in the discussions with his mother-in-law, but the account suggests that the parting was not expected to occur when and where it did, just short of a difficult and dangerous stretch of the route where his company and escort might have been particularly needed. As it was, he and his men turned back to Lichfield while his lady, with a company of 10 persons and 13 horses, went on to Derby 'with a heavy heart, considering how many things stood between my Lord and I'. The passage of the Dangerous Moors, 'where never coach went before mine', was accomplished with considerable difficulty, as the horses had sometimes to be taken out and the coach man-handled down the hills, and one of the escort-horses, ridden by Rivers, her gentleman-usher,

---

*So here, and in the list of the establishment at Knole, but probably identifiable with the Judith Shrimpton of later references, Lady Anne is not consistent in her spelling of proper names, especially those of her household.

fell off a bridge into the river, but the little party got to Manchester at ten at night on 1 March.

After that, the Knole diary is silent for something over a fortnight. If, as appears most likely, it is an attempt at a detailed record of Lady Anne's fight for her inheritance, this is very easy to understand. Sixty years later she was able to recall the remaining stages of the journey, by way of Chorley (where the lodging was so bad that she broke her custom of resting on Sunday and went on rather than stay there for another night), through Preston, Lancaster and Kendal, arriving at Brougham on the 6th. A week later she went to Naworth for a couple of nights to stay with the Howards, and saw Carlisle Castle and the Cathedral, where her great-grandfather Lord Dacres was buried, but all this was beside the purpose of the document at Knole. She would have no need to remind herself, and other people would have no business to know, of those last few weeks in her mother's company, in the county which meant so much to them. For a little while, at any rate, their pressing problem could be laid aside, for they were of one mind, and knew it.

But under the arrangement made at Dorset House, Lady Anne had to give her answer by the 22nd of the month. On the 20th the diary begins again with the arrival of their equivocal neighbour Lord William Howard and his son to take back that answer, and it was a direct denial. The interview seems to have been a stormy one, as Sir Timothy Whittington arrived the same day and, as Lady Anne puts it, 'did all he could do to mitigate the anger between my Lord *William Howard* and my Mother, so as at last we parted all good friends'. It looks as if there had been a peremptory summons to her and her entourage to come back to London at once, but it was finally arranged that they should have another 10 days or so in the north and all go to London after Easter, which fell on the last day of the month. This interview must have done much to show Lady Anne that her mother had not been far wrong in her reluctance to put much reliance on Lord William Howard. On the face of it, however,

the two families remained on friendly terms, and next
week Lord William's son sent over a dapple-grey saddle-
horse from Naworth for the use of his cousin Anne.

Things were not going too well at present for the
Howard family. It will be remembered that Frances
Howard, Lord William's niece and Dorset's first cousin,
had lately been the central figure in a rather discreditable
divorce-case, and had married the King's current favourite
Robert Carr, in spite of the opposition of his close friend
Sir Thomas Overbury. Since then Carr had been raised to
the earldom of Somerset. Overbury had been sent to the
Tower out of harm's way, and had already died there,
probably of poison, the Lieutenant of the Tower had been
hanged for it, and now came the sudden accusation that
it was Lady Somerset who had had it done. She was
arraigned for murder, and on the 24th of the month was
sent by water to the Tower. Lady Anne noted this date
in the margin of her diary at this point, but John
Chamberlain, writing in early April, says it was on the
27th. (He adds that she was to have been quartered in
the lodging that Overbury himself had occupied, but
pleaded so passionately and desperately against it that
the new Lieutenant had to move out of his own apartments and let her stay there until Ralegh's former rooms
could be got ready for her, Sir Walter having been released
a week before.)

Meanwhile, mother and daughter remained at Brougham
and made an expedition in a coach to Whinfell Park to
see the woods, which by this time would be coming out
in their first spring green. A few days later the saddle-
horse arrived for Lady Anne's use, and on the 31st of the
month she and Lady Cumberland made their Easter
communion in the chapel at Brougham. Next day they
heard how the decision had been received in London.
Lord Charles Howard, a brother of the newly-arrested
Lady Somerset, arrived with Lord Dorset's instructions.
He wanted his coach, his horses and his servants in London,
and they were to come back at once, but he did *not* want
his wife, and they were specifically told to return without

her. He was quite obviously furious, and it looked as
if the threatened separation had come at last. Lady
Cumberland was indignant, and spoke her mind freely,
but for little Lady Anne it may well have been a momentary relief that the moment of confrontation with her
husband was at least postponed. The older woman,
however, would perceive another point. If Lord Dorset's
instructions were followed implicitly, without question,
it would be easy for him to claim, and for people in the
south to believe, that it was his lady who had deserted
him, and that the blame for the separation was to be laid
at her door. To guard against that, a paper was drawn up,
signed by Lady Anne and countersigned by all the
gentlemen present, setting out that she both desired and
offered to go to London with the men and horses, but
that by her husband's express command they would not
consent to her doing so. She had done what she could to
safeguard herself against any subsequent charge of disobedience or desertion, and the cavalcade set off from
Brougham, leaving her behind.

All the same, that piece of documentary justification
was not likely to carry much weight in the estimation of
people in general. The actual fact of the separation, and
of her stay in the north, self-appointed or otherwise, would
be evident to a far wider circle of friends, acquaintances
and miscellaneous gossips than would ever have the
opportunity, or take the trouble, to enquire about the
rights and wrongs of it, and it would do no good to her
husband or herself. She and her mother had slept together
and talked far into the night about the position, and it
must have been clear to both of them that an open breach
was to be avoided at all costs. Coach, horses and servants
had left for London without their mistress, and to that
extent their master's orders had been obeyed, but there
was no saying how long he would remain in the same
mind. Quite possibly he might have come already to
regret his rash, ill-tempered order, with its public slight
upon his lady, and would have still more cause to regret
it when her absence was generally known, but by that

time the mischief would have been done, and the news
of the separation would have come hard on the heels
of the other family scandal. With his cousin suddenly
clapped in the Tower for murder, and his wife apparently
banished to the Border for no explicit reason, he would
find it hard indeed to keep up the life of fashionable
easy-going popularity that meant so much to him. Lord
Charles would be embarrassingly conscious of this when
he brought the order, and the escort when they obeyed it.
The situation was getting worse and worse.

But things could not be allowed to go on like this.
Their wrong-headed course had to be stopped, and it
was Lady Anne who stopped it. By letting the men and
horses take the road for the south, as ordered, she had
avoided open defiance on her part, and open disobedience
on theirs, but that same night she sent two messengers
after them (there was safety in numbers in that wild
countryside, especially after dark) asking them to wait,
as she was coming with them after all. Next day, the
2nd of April, she set out, riding with her mother in
the latter's coach. It was natural that they should make the
most of every moment they could have together, for
there was a strong possibility that they might never
see each other again, and as a matter of fact they never
did. We know, through Lady Anne's action in later
years, just how far they went, and why. For something
over half a mile from Brougham the way is level and
reasonably straightforward going, but there comes a
point where the old Roman road plunges abruptly down-
wards and begins a series of hill-and-dale undulations
that no cumbrous Jacobean coach could venture upon,
except in absolute necessity, and certainly not when
it would have to turn round and be dragged uphill again
almost at once. When mother and daughter got to the
brow of the hill they must have known, both of
them, that this was the end. The coach was stopped, and
by the roadside they had 'a grievous and heavy parting',
and eventually Lady Anne rode on alone, quite possibly
on the grey saddle-horse that her cousin William had

sent her. One or more of her mother's people would probably bear her company till she caught up with her own servants, and would then be able to take back the grey if, as seems possible, it had been a loan and would have to be returned ultimately to Naworth. For Lady Cumberland, when once her daughter was out of sight, there was only a slow reversal of the coach and a lonely journey back to Brougham, now doubly desolate, for what was left of her life.

There is another blank in the diary for about a week. We know only that for most of the way Lady Anne rode pillion behind a Mr. Hodgson, one of the gentlemen in attendance, and that on the 10th of April they were met at Tottenham by Lord Dorset's coach with its escort of mounted men, and eventually came to London, to Little Dorset House. These details have a significance of their own, and must have done much to relieve the apprehensions of Lady Anne. Whatever their relations in private, there was not to be an immediate public breach between husband and wife; the presence of the coach would show as much to everyone, and it would not be generally seen that its noble owner was not within it. The Earl and Countess of Dorset were both returning to town in full state, as they had set out, and this, socially speaking, was important. William Shakespeare, then in the last fortnight of his life, had unconsciously shown the attitude of the time in two of his Roman plays not many years before. Octavius Caesar in *Antony and Cleopatra,* and the friends of Tullus Aufidius in the last act of *Coriolanus,* had in their several ways made that clear enough. A person of quality was expected to arrive in some degree of state, and an unexpected entry, if not made in preparation for a spectacular *coup d'état,* was merely poor-spirited and rather low. Aufidius is accused of entering his native town as meanly as a post-boy, and Octavius, in welcoming his injured sister, is indignant with Antony not only for having deserted her for Cleopatra, but for letting her come 'a market-maid to Rome', without the attendance and publicity due to her birth and present station. Any neglect of proper ceremony was looked upon as a calculated slight, and it was a possibility that cannot have been far from the minds of Lady Anne and her attendants. That formal, empty welcome must have relieved them, however, and next day they went down to Knole.

Here their reception was rather less encouraging. Lord Dorset did not show himself anywhere about. He may have been out, he may have been busy with company, he may have been merely sulking, but among all the bustle of his lady's return from the north he made no effort to go and meet her. On the other hand, her beloved little daughter Margaret, a baby not yet two years old, was waiting for her at the outermost gate, and that was much. The passionate mother-and-daughter affection, that had wept itself out not ten days before on the roadside at Brougham, was gaining new life from the reminder that that daughter had a daughter of her own.

Eventually 'my Lord came to me in the Drawing Chamber', probably full of disapproval. For one thing, his lady had not agreed to the capitulation, but had sided with her mother against him; for another, she had taken matters into her own hands and come back in defiance of his instructions; for yet another, she had contrived by doing so, to avoid precipitating a family crisis at a time when his family had enough on their minds already, so that he could not help feeling a certain relief and a kind of grudging gratitude, which he would not like at all. She had done the right thing, flatly against his orders, and they were both the better for it. And, when all was said and done, they were both very fond of each other and, in most matters, proud of each other into the bargain, and they were still in their 'twenties. It was a combination of circumstances and emotions that would naturally make him very cross.

Whatever they spoke of, it was no time, after all that journeying, to talk much about the main matter, but on the following day, the 12th, Dorset got down to business,

and demanded that his lady should sign and seal, without
more ado, her formal acceptance of the award made
against her by the Court. He would think that he was
master of the last trick of the game, but Lady Anne
had another card to play. The documents might be all
made out ready for signature, but she could not sign
them, nevertheless, because she had not got them with
her. They were now in her mother's hands at Brougham,
so the question of her own consent or refusal did not
arise. The fact was simple and unanswerable, and Dorset
went up to London, probably in a rage, to see what could
be done next.

After that, there came a period of uncertainty and
apprehension. The next thing, presumably, would be a
summons to London for further confrontations, but it
did not come. On the 17th Tom Woodgate, the Yeoman
of the Great Chamber, came back to Knole, but brought
no message with him. Next day came one of the senior
officials, Peter Baskett, Lord Dorset's Gentleman of the
Horse, with a letter from his master asking peremptorily,
for the last time, whether Lady Anne would agree,
in writing, to accept the award of the judges. Wretched
but indomitable, she wrote back on the morrow that
she would not do so, 'what misery soever it cost me'.
She never admitted to being ill, but now she seems to have
kept to her room, if not her bed, as she notes that her
child and the Bishop of St. David's were 'brought to
speak to her' on that particular day. The bishop was at
that time a neighbour; earlier in the year Lord and Lady
Dorset had gone to church at Sevenoaks when he was
preaching there, he had kept Lady Anne company in her
carriage on her next journey to London, and at a later
period he was to go to the north when translated to the
see of Carlisle.

And so the spring days dragged on. It was getting
light earlier and earlier in the mornings, and she was able
to begin the day by taking her prayer-book out into the
garden, away from contact with any of her household,
and imploring her Maker to be merciful and help her

'as he always hath done' in all the difficulties that
confronted her.

The gardens at Knole are comparatively little changed,
even now, from what they were in her time, and the
place known nowadays as 'the Duchess's seat' is generally
understood to be that referred to in the diary as the
'Standing', and habitually used by her as a kind of open-air
oratory in those days of her distress.

Presently there came further news to upset her, from
the north. Lady Cumberland had been taken ill, on her
way from service in the castle chapel at Brougham, and
was suddenly attacked with a pain in her side, from what
seems most likely to have been pleurisy. Messengers took
their time to cover the distance of the rugged northern
roads, and there must have been nerve-racking periods of
anxiety between one bulletin and the next. Later on,
however, the news was more encouraging, and towards the
end of the month a still extant letter shows that Lady
Anne is expressing thankfulness for her mother's improvement in health, and sending her the latest news about the
baby. At the same time she takes every opportunity of
showing her husband in the best possible light, and paying
ready tribute to his generosity, thoughtfulness, tenderness
and affectionate conduct in all matters except this one of
the inheritance, over which they are all so regrettably at
odds. The letter is irrefutable evidence of her unwavering
loyalty to him and her refusal to admit any general
disparagement of him, even from the mother whom
she adored.

April came to an end, and still there was no sign, but
with the opening of May things began to happen. On
May-Day itself, in the afternoon, serious tidings were
brought to her by one 'Rivers', probably the gentleman-
usher who had that misfortune with the horse, but just
possibly Sir George Rivers, her husband's friend and
business adviser and ultimately executor of his will. She
was to live no longer at Knole nor at their mansion of
Bolebrook. No doubt some suitable place would be found
for her where she could live in obscurity (as if she had

misconducted herself and ceased to be socially acceptable)
but her husband no longer wanted her as chatelaine of
his houses and hostess of his guests. It was a slight, and a
grave one, but not, perhaps, so over-whelmingly crushing
as Lord Dorset meant it to be, because though unwelcome
it was not unfamiliar. As a little girl she had been through
it all before, when her father and mother were not on
speaking terms, and those days of childhood were not as
yet so very far off. Even now she was only 26, and she had
seen, by the example of her parents, how these moments
of passionate insult and injury could pass, and the warring
parties be brought together again. On the very next day
Mr. Edward Legge, her husband's steward, arrived from
London and mentioned to some of the servants that their
master would be arriving shortly to see his lady, but it
would be for the last time, as they were on the point of
parting for ever. Here, too, the threat would be less
terrifying than was intended. Lady Anne had a better
opinion of her husband, and a stronger confidence in
his feeling for her, than his conduct at the moment was
likely to suggest.

There was another thing, however, that Lord Dorset
could do to strengthen his own position and intensify
her anxiety and distress, and in this extremity he did
it. He sent Baskett for the child. Once again his continued
and genuine affection for his wife, and their common love
for the little Lady Margaret, showed him where he could
strike to hurt, and he was not wrong, for this demand
brought her very near to breaking-point. She momentarily
thought of flat disobedience and refusal to comply; then,
like the mother who contended for her child before
King Solomon, she resolutely put the child's welfare
before her own. It was better that she herself should
suffer the pain of parting, and the desolation that would
follow, than that her own conduct should make trouble
for them all, and particularly between Margaret and her
father. It would not be fair, to make her an innocent
sharer in her mother's insubordination, so with a heavy
heart she complied. She sent for Legge, had a long and

tearful conversation with him, and the arrangements were made.

Once again, though almost certainly without knowing it, she had taken the trick. There had been three courses before her, and either of the other two would have played into her husband's hands. To have defied and disobeyed him would have put her unquestionably in the wrong over one important matter, and it would have been hard to convince the world that she was in the right over another. The remaining course—to have capitulated and promised to sign anything, and agree to anything, provided that she could keep her child—was what Dorset is most likely to have expected and hoped for, but from her own account of the matter it simply does not seem to have occurred to her. Like a dutiful wife—as indeed she was—she had obeyed her lord; he had got what he asked for, but he was as far as ever from getting what he really wanted.

But meanwhile there had been other tribulations. The child duly arrived at Great Dorset House, and her father decided that she should live at Horsley in future, and never go back to Knole. Two days later Lady Anne had another long talk with Edward Legge, who had superintended the little girl's journey to London, and gave him a clearer impression of the whole position, leaving him with a better understanding of her own point of view. The same evening, however, she had another setback. Another visitor arrived at Knole, and she was confronted with the unwelcome presence of Lord Dorset's confidant and favourite, Mr. Matthew Caldicott. He brought the ring that had been used at the marriage of her husband's grandparents, and the message that the child was not, after all, to go to Horsley just yet, but that Dorset himself would be coming down to Knole in the following week. This sounded a little more encouraging, and it may have some relation to the fact that just then, in sporting and fashionable circles, Dorset was doing rather well. He had just won over £200 at a cocking-match, and Lord Essex and Lord Willoughby had backed his fancy, to their own great advantage. Altogether, he was in high favour and, it would seem, in correspondingly good spirits. His lady sent him their own wedding-ring in return for the one he had sent down to her by Matthew, but there is nothing to suggest that he had asked for it. In all likelihood it was a gesture of unsolicited surrender on her part, inspired by her reading of Chaucer. The events of the third and fifth sections of the Clerk of Oxford's Tale, culminating in the surrender of the wedding-ring, bore a distinct relation to those of the last few days, and she can hardly be blamed if she saw herself as a contemporary Patient Griselda, and made a spontaneous gesture to emphasise the resemblance and to counteract the impression, held by many of her neighbours, that she was being obstinate and unreasonable in not falling in with her husband's wishes.

That view was held even by some of her own household. Marsh, her personal attendant, urged her to consent to the proposed agreement, probably for her own sake, and on the 14th a messenger from London brought her a letter from Matthew Caldicott that contained something like a threat. She was to submit to her husband's wishes without further delay, or she would be 'undone for ever'. The favourite's influence with his master seems to have been at its height at this time; when Dorset came down in a day or two, and had a discussion with his lady about the whole business, Matthew stayed in the room with them all the while, and seems to have taken part in the argument. Such, at any rate, is the impression one gains from Lady Anne's words 'we all fell out, and so parted for that night'.

Eventually it was agreed that Marsh should go at once to Brougham with a letter from Lady Anne embodying a new proposal. The dowager should make over her jointure at once to Dorset, but he would give her an annual rent for it. Dorset went back to London, Lady Anne prepared the letters as required, and sent them up unsealed, so that her husband could read them first and see that she was keeping her word.

Matters appeared to be getting a little easier. The baby had gone down to West Horsley to the Comptons, and the Beauchamps were staying there at the same time. Lady Compton and Lady Beauchamp were sisters of Lord Dorset, and it was apparently a matter of some relief to Lady Anne to know that the child was with both her aunts. Finally, and probably most welcome news of all, Rivers the usher came from London and brought word that Lady Cumberland was reported to be very much better. The chief piece of news on the other side of the family was that Lady Somerset had been brought to trial in Westminster Hall for instigating Overbury's murder, had pleaded guilty and had thrown herself upon the King's mercy, shedding occasional tears and winning the sympathy of the bystanders. Her husband came up for trial the next day and denied everything, but was nevertheless found guilty. Both were condemned to death, but the sentence was commuted to imprisonment in the Tower, and they were eventually pardoned when the matter had blown over. Chamberlain's letters give a clear indication that the whole affair was a great social event, being attended, in his words, by 'more Ladies and other great personages than ever I think were seen at any trial', but at last it was over, and Dorset and his friends could leave London for Buckhurst on their way to a festival of assorted sporting fixtures at Lewes.

Meanwhile, local opinion was apparently changing. Lady Selby, of Ightham Mote, came to call, and reported that people were now being heard to say that Lady Anne had done well in not agreeing to the compromise her husband had so urgently required. To Lady Anne, desolate and deserted in the great house which she had been told was no longer to be her home, that little piece of friendly gossip was a welcome relief, and was duly noted in her diary, but next day there came one Kendall from Brougham with very sorrowful news. The previous week's good report must have been premature, if it was not a device of Dorset's to get his lady into a more amenable frame of mind, for the chill and pleurisy had run their course, and Lady Cumberland was dead. Her will, which Kendall had brought with him, contained a clause that caused her daughter additional distress, for it enjoined that her body should be buried in the parish church of Alnwick in Northumberland, where her brother Francis already lay. In view of the family dissensions, it was natural that she should have no desire to rest in the Cliffords' vault at Skipton, but to Lady Anne it was 'a sign that I should be dispossessed of the inheritance of my forefathers'.

There was much to be done, as there always is at such a time. Another of the household, one Hamon, was sent off that same night to carry the news, and the will, to Lord Dorset at Lewes. Next day the bishop of St. David's called to comfort Lady Anne in her bereavement, and in the afternoon she sent for her neighbour Sir William Selby to consult him about ways and means of sending her mother's body to Alnwick, and the possibility of building a little memorial chapel. These last plans proved unnecessary, however, for on the following day, Friday, 31 May, came messages from different quarters. Lord Dorset sent to say that he would be arriving on the Saturday, and a letter from Lady Anne's own attendant Woolridge, just then at Brougham, brought the news that there had been a codicil to the will, directing that Lady Cumberland's body should be buried where 'her deare and noble sole dau. and heire, should think fitt'. That, at least, was some consolation.

Chapter Five

LADY ANNE AT BROUGHAM

The quarrel is between our masters, and us their men.
Romeo and Juliet, I, i

LADY CUMBERLAND'S death radically changed matters for her son-in-law. There was no longer any question of arranging, for a consideration, the ultimate disposal of the jointure-lands to the Cliffords; if he were not quick and careful, they would move in as natural heirs, without having to pay him anything at all, so he came down firmly and instantly on the side of his wife. He was with her by seven in the morning on the Saturday, having risen early and left his fashionable company at Lewes, and though he went to bed at once and slept till mid-day, they were busy enough in the afternoon. Rivers was set to writing letters for Lady Anne's signature to various people in the north, including Ralph Coniston, one of her mother's executors, Sir Christopher Pickering an old family friend who was looking after the property, and Woolridge, who was still at Brougham. They were formally notified that Lord Dorset was taking possession of the estate by right of his wife, and that Lady Cumberland's body was to be wrapped in lead at once, pending further instructions. Then, at four o'clock, the earl set off for London, taking Rivers with him. The initial step had been taken, and it was an important one. The Cliffords might put in their claim, but for the moment Lady Anne, with the support of her husband, had got in first. Three days later, Rivers and Marsh came back from London with the welcome news that Dorset had quarrelled with Lord William Howard and had taken Counsel's opinion, and had written to Westmorland in consequence, confirming Lady Anne's instructions and enjoining Lady Cumberland's servants and tenants to keep possession of the property in the name of himself and his wife. For the moment at least the rival heirs were held in check, which was, as Lady Anne put it, 'a thing I little expected but which gave me much contentment'.

The Cliffords, or their representatives, had found that on this occasion they were a day after the fair. It was hardly expected that they could march in and take possession at Brougham, where the dead Countess lay unburied, in her leaden shroud, but they made a forcible entry into Appleby Castle, breaking open doors and windows and expelling Lord Dorset's agents who had just moved in, as instructed, to see to the safe keeping of the building itself and such of Lady Cumberland's goods as were stored there. Dorset was naturally indignant, and took action at once. He seems to have got the ear of the King and the Privy Council, because a few days later Rivers and a companion were sent down to Westmorland with letters from the Council to the Justices of the Peace, enjoining them to see that things were left undisturbed as they had been at the time of their late owner's death. until. the question of ownership and inheritance had been officially decided. Lord Cumberland had to apologise, explaining that he had thought Dorset was going to accept the proposed compromise, and that nobody had been living at Appleby for the past two years except the Dorset's recent emissaries. He had sent his son to see just what was happening, and it looks very much as if it were the younger man, notoriously impetuous and dynamic, who had decided to make a bold stroke for the property and had put himself and his party in the wrong by doing so.

By this time husband and wife were both in London, at Great Dorset House, and very soon the pressure began again, though with a different object. The recent actions of both parties had made it unlikely that Dorset would be able to get anything out of his wife's uncle and cousin by helping them to a peaceful enjoyment of the Westmorland property, so the best thing to do, in his view, was to play for a higher stake still, and get it for himself.

He could not always count on a continuous run of luck at the cockpit or on the racecourse, and money must be found somehow. If he could gain absolute possession of the estates, he could lease them, or in extremity even sell them—to the Cliffords or to anyone else, if he could find a purchaser who would offer a better price—and for a while, at any rate, he would be financially on his feet again. The trouble was that they were not his to sell, and everybody knew it. He had himself made the point that they were, or should be, his wife's property by inheritance, and that was not quite the same thing. Anything done in that line would have to be done with her consent, and he set himself assiduously to get it.

First of all he made it a family matter, alleging that it would be well for Lady Anne to transfer her rights in the property to him and to the child. This was rather too transparent to be acceptable. The little girl's rights, in her minority, would be vested in her father, who could do what he liked with the property and claim to be administering it for her own good, and her mother would then be powerless to stop him. Quite naturally, she would not agree. Lord William Howard, her old opponent, was brought in to persuade—or possibly browbeat—her into compliance, but she was still unalterably resolute. Then, by the end of the day, Dorset must have lost his temper, for at half an hour's notice he packed her off to Knole.

She left her London home at eight o'clock in the evening, with only one woman in attendance. It was mid-June, so that there would not have been too many hours of darkness on the road, but even so, it must have been an exhausting journey, after the strain and passion that had preceded it, and the little party did not reach Knole till midnight. Once there, Lady Anne seems to have concentrated her attention on something quite different, and set herself down to intensive domestic embroidery. Legge the steward came down from London and had 'much talk', and it looks as if they had drafted, between them, an acceptable amendment, because two days later a small party came down to wait upon her, bringing the deed of conveyance for her to see. There was Peter Baskett from her husband, and with him Dr. Layfield and Ralph Coniston, two of her mother's executors. The proposal was that she should return to London and sign the agreement with her husband before a Justice, and though she would not consent, the reason she gave for her refusal is significant enough. She resented the way she had been sent down so abruptly, only two days earlier, but there is no suggestion that she objected in any way to the deed in its correct form. She was not going to come running at her lord's call just because he had got over his ill-temper, and Dr. Layfield must have gone back next day to report as much, because when he returned on the day after that, Lord Dorset came with him, to ask for his lady's compliance instead of commanding her obedience. Her memorandum notes that 'my Lord persuaded me to consent to his business and assured me how kind and good a husband he would be to me'. On both sides it was an honourable capitulation.

Back they went to London on the following day, with Dr. Layfield and Lady Anne's attendant Katharine, and the deed was officially signed, conveying the Westmorland inheritance to Dorset *if Lady Anne should have no descendants surviving her.* That alteration made all the difference. Dorset had provisional expectations of the property—which would in some degree restore his financial standing among his creditors—but that was all. While little Lady Margaret lived, her mother was still in possession. Letters were written at once to Lord William Howard to tell him of the arrangement, and Marsh was sent off with them, and with instructions to take particular care for the safe keeping of Brougham. Dorset went down on a day's visit to Horsley to see the child, and Lady Anne went visiting elsewhere on her own, calling on Lord Knollys, who had apartments in the Tilt-yard at Whitehall, and having her first sight of her little namesake Lady Anne Carr, the six-month-old baby of the imprisoned Countess of Somerset. Her husband was soon back, the two of them went to church together at St. Bride's on the Sunday, and next day they took the barge to Greenwich (a very different experience, at midsummer, from that February river-journey where Lady Anne had caught such a bad cold) to attend the King and Queen at the service in the palace chapel. After dinner with her mother's kinsfolk the Bedfords, they went up to the gallery and were received by the Queen, whom they found particularly kind. Their family difficulties would be well known by this time in fashionable circles, and as they were both well liked it must have given genuine pleasure in many quarters to see them together again.

Further news came from the north, and it was agreed that Lady Anne had better go up there as soon as possible, not only for her mother's funeral but to be seen and known there as the new owner and occupier of the property. She went down again to Greenwich to take formal leave of the Queen and her personal friends at Court—and of Lady Knollys, who was disagreeable to her and was answered in kind—and came back to find her husband most helpful and considerate. He arranged that the child's present attendant Mrs. Bathurst, who was proving somehow unsatisfactory, should be replaced by the faithful Mrs. Willoughby until Lady Anne should make other arrangements, he promised faithfully to join her in the north as soon as he could and that when this was over the child should come back to her. The winter of her discontent was indeed made glorious summer by this reconciliation, and as June came to an end she recorded happily in her diary that 'my Lord and I were never greater friends than at this time'.

Everything now ran smoothly, even though Dorset lost '200 twenty shilling pieces' by betting on the running powers of Acton Curvett, his chief footman. This may well explain a hasty last-minute arrangement by which his lady, on the very morning of her departure, signed a deed making over to him a great part of the allowance due to her under their marriage settlement, under his 'faithful word and promise' that she should have her full entitlement in the coming Michaelmas term. Chief Justice Hobart

came to Dorset House to supervise the arrangement,
and about one o'clock on that day, 1 July, she set
forth again for Westmorland, her husband seeing her
down to the door of the coach, where they had 'a
loving and kind parting'. For the first time she was going
as ruler of her little northern kingdom, to take possession
of her inheritance.

There was a slight set-back, however, as soon as she got
there. Her mother's body had been duly prepared for
burial, but on 11 July came word that 'it could not
be buried at Appleby'. Rivers was sent off at once and
got what the diary calls 'their consents', but there is no
indication who 'they' are, or what the objection had been.
The peculiarly independent position of Appleby, however,
may well provide the answer. Though the old township of
Bongate, on the Brougham side of the river, was part of the
Clifford estates, Appleby itself was not. Small as it was, it
had been established as a royal borough in the days of
Henry II, and a hundred years later it had successfully
resisted an attempt to treat it as an appendage of the
castle. Its overlord was not Vipont or Clifford, but the
King, and its governors were the borough officers, as
being set in authority under him. Only some 20 years
before, an Elizabethan pamphleteer (probably Jervas
Markham, a member of a still-extant Westmorland family)
had referred, respectfully but not over-seriously, to the
deference accorded to 'the Lord Maior of Applebie
within his whole limit, precinct or corporation', and
though it was one of the smallest boroughs in England,
that was no reason why it should be ignored, or taken
for granted. It was in the church of Bongate, not of
Appleby, that a former Lady Clifford had been buried,
though her tomb had been dismembered and forgotten
in the image-hating days of the Reformation, and her
15th-century effigy lay walled up in the stonework, not
to be discovered for another two centuries and a half.
Appleby would readily accord the dead Countess a resting-
place within the church of the borough if it were asked,
but it would not welcome too ready an assumption, by

those in charge at Brougham, that it could be had as a right, without the formality of asking.

This was just the sort of argument that would appeal to Lady Anne. Tenacious of her own rights, she could understand and appreciate other people's, particularly when they had their roots in the ancient history of the locality and local families, and there is no trace, in her account, of reluctance or resentment. There was a favour to be asked, and she asked for it accordingly, and it was granted. That was all, and the funeral could go forward as arranged. Lord William Howard came over from Naworth about five o'clock, with five or six companions, there was a pause for rest and refreshment of men and horses. and at eight the procession set out on the 10-mile journey to Appleby through the summer night. For the last time Lady Cumberland's coach, with Lady Cumberland in it, went out through the gates of Brougham along the road she and her daughter had travelled only a few months before, but this time there was no pause for parting and return. The coach and its four horses went on, down the hill with Lady Anne following in her own coach and pair. Most of the men and women, she says, were on horseback, but they would naturally go at a walking pace, and the company, some 40 strong, got to Appleby about half-past eleven. All was in readiness, by midnight the body was laid in its grave in the sanctuary, and at three in the morning they returned to Brougham. Lady Anne wrote a letter to her husband—presumably an account of the proceedings and her own plans in regard to the property—and let Lord William see it before it went.

As usual, she showed herself sensible and discreet. A few days after the funeral she rode into Whinfell Park and saw some of her tenants. It was high summer, and they were getting in their hay. This was something that had to be done while the fine weather lasted, no matter whose tenants they turned out to be, but she was in no hurry to press for payments of the customary fines due to a new landlord succeeding to the estates. That would be best left to await an official ruling, and she told them therefore to keep the money 'till it was known who had a right to it', She was not going to prejudice her position by asking for or accepting money until she had been fully established in her entitlement. Exercising authority was another matter, however, and just a fortnight after the funeral she signed her first warrant for the killing of a stag in the Forest of Stainmore.

Her uncle's people were less discreet. At the end of the month they interrupted the work of haymaking in Brougham Park itself and met with sturdy resistance on the part of a Mr. Kidd, who wounded one of them in the leg and another in the foot. It looks as if they had gone arbitrarily into the field on horseback, and the valiant Mr. Kidd had laid about him with a hay-rake—or perhaps even a pitchfork—the legs and feet of a mounted man being particularly vulnerable to an adversary on the ground. There were instant and indignant complaints made at Carlisle, and the Justices issued a warrant for Lady Anne's haymakers to be arrested and bound over to come up for trial at Kendal at the forthcoming Assizes.

It did not come to that, however. Three days later, on 1 August, the judges paused at Brougham on their way from Carlisle to Kendal, saw Lady Anne and investigated the matter. The case was summarily dismissed on the spot, the defendants were released and relieved of their obligation to appear, and on the following Monday her cousin-by-courtesy, John Dudley, came to supper and reported that her actions and explanations had been very well spoken of. Obviously the new landowner was finding acceptance and approval among her neighbours, and a week later, Marsh arrived from London with still more welcome news. King James had signed an order that she was to remain in undisturbed possession of Brougham Castle for the present, her husband would be coming up to Brougham himself very shortly, and meanwhile everything was going well. Her cousin, Lady Somerset, had had her death sentence commuted to one of imprisonment, and she and her husband were enjoying a measure of social life in the Tower. On the whole, the fortunes of the Howards were again in the ascendant.

Lord Dorset arrived on the 22nd, 'with a great company of horses', and Lady Anne went to meet him at Appleby Town's End, bearing him and Lord William Howard company in the coach on the way back to Brougham. His party formed the vanguard; some of the servants arrived later in the evening, but even so, they got to Brougham ahead of the luggage and furniture that customarily accompanied the household on its journeys, so that night they had to sleep three or four in a bed. People of quality, when they travelled from one estate to another, took with them their personal furniture and belongings, the progress being something like that of an army on the move. Accordingly, when the luggage-train arrived, it took some days to 'dress the house' throughout. The room over the gatehouse, where Lady Cumberland had died and where her body had lain in state among draperies of black, was adorned at once with fresh hangings, the Dorsets' green velvet bed was set up there, and that night Lady Anne had the satisfaction of lying beside her husband in the state bedroom of her own castle. They were together again, and on affectionate terms as of old. He had brought along his will and showed it to her, and she saw with surprise and pleasure that while a certain annual sum was to go to his brother, and another was set aside for the payment of his debts, the whole of his estate, save for her own jointure, was settled upon their child.

It was obviously a source of mild satisfaction that when her cousin Lord Clifford arrived at Appleby a few days later it was 'with a far less train than my Lord'. There was a little trouble just after that, and the account in the Knole manuscript is tantalisingly ambiguous. 'Upon the 27th our folks being all at ——' and then comes a blank —— 'there passed some ill words betwixt *Matthew,* one of the Keepers, and *William Durin,* whereupon they fell to blows and . . . made a great uproar in the town'.

The town in question is most likely to have been Appleby, but there would hardly be any uncertainty about its name. The statement that 'our folks were all at' anything shows that it was a gathering of some sort, presumably a sporting one like a bull-baiting (the ring for which is still to be seen in Appleby market-place), an archery contest in the butts behind the church, or a horse-race just across the river. Perhaps the 18th-century copyist could not read Lady Anne's writing at this point, or Lady Anne herself was not sure, at the time, what that particular entertainment was, and left the blank to be filled in afterwards. The other doubtful point is the number, and identity, of the people who began the quarrel. William Durin may have fallen out with a keeper named Matthew, but the name by itself, elsewhere in the diary, always denotes Matthew Caldicott, Dorset's 'favourite' and hanger-on. That unpleasant person from London could easily have given offence to one or more of the Westmorland servants, especially as a sporting contest always gave scope for widespread betting, arguing, and the airing of personal judgements. The gathering would include not only the Dorsets' men but probably some of Lord Clifford's, quite apart from its normal complement of Appleby townspeople and interested spectators from the surrounding villages. Mr. Edwards, the secretary and Mr. Grosvenor the gentleman-usher drew their swords, presumably to part the original combatants, but three or four people were wounded, and someone who went off to ring the alarm-bell, which hung in its bell-cote over the gable of the Moot Hall, fell off the ladder and was badly hurt. It is all very like the opening of *Romeo and Juliet,* but appears to have stopped short of intervention by authority. Possibly the injury of one man by accident, rather than by anyone's personal assault, brought matters to a standstill, as we hear no more of what might have developed into a serious affray. On the contrary, the next day seems to have been particularly peaceful. The dressing of the house was finished in the morning, and Lady Anne spent the afternoon at her embroidery, while her husband sat by her and read. The note of it in her diary suggests a deep contentment.

This way of life was obviously more to her taste than to her husband. For a man of his interests and connections it was exile in comparison with country life as lived at Knole or Bolebrook, where he could keep in touch with country sports at Lewes or fashionable entertainments at Whitehall. He spent about a fortnight in the north, including a visit to his Howard cousins at Naworth, and by mid-September he was back in London, leaving his lady to establish her position by continued residence on the disputed property. She wanted to join him in London, and wrote 'a very earnest letter' asking permission to do so, but in 10 days' time Rivers arrived with a reply that she was to stay where she was for the winter. This need not mean that they were once more at odds; it is more likely that the Clifford family constituted a threat to the peaceful possession of the estate. King James's order ensured that Lady Anne should remain undisturbed at Brougham while the matter was being decided, but it would lose most of its force if the Cliffords could claim that she was an absentee.

If the property were left unoccupied at this critical time, it would be very easy for the Cumberland faction to move in and say that it had been neglected, and that they were looking after it for its own good. They had done that prematurely in the summer with Appleby Castle, before Lady Anne had gone to the north at all, and though they had had to move out of it at the command of the Privy Council, they might claim justification for doing it at Brougham if the claimant was not in residence to care for what she maintained was her property. While the matter was *sub judice,* possession was nine points of the law, and therefore possession must be rigorously maintained.

All the same, Lady Anne must have found this continued residence very dull. The things for which she really cared were her child, whom she had not

seen for months, her husband, whose recent kindness
had made him increasingly dear to her, and her succession
to the inheritance of her fathers, and she had no means
of really knowing how that matter was getting on. The
Knole manuscript shows itself to be essentially an account
of the struggle for the succession rather than a daily
register of events, because for a whole month, at this
point, there is nothing recorded at all. The September
entries are few enough, and after that message from
Rivers, cutting short all hopes of a winter in London, there
comes an entry that is rather difficult to date.

> Upon the 31st I rid into *Whinfield* in the afternoon.
> This month I spent in working and reading. Mr. *Dumbell*
> read a great part of the *History of the Netherlands.*

Something rather peculiar has happened here. This
paragraph closes the September entries, but there is no
such date in the calendar, September having no more
than 30 days even in Leap Year. Has Lady Anne, or
the copyist, written 31st when it should have been 30th,
or has a cross-heading been left out, referring it to
October? The latter explanation would give point to the
second sentence, making it a realisation that the end
of the month had come and nothing worth recording
had happened at all. This fits in with the general impression of frustration and near-stagnation given by the
entries at this time, but one cannot rule out the possibility
that the 18th-century copyist may have turned over two
pages in transcribing the lost original, or simply ended
one days' work with the preceding September entry and
mistaken his starting-point when taking the work in
hand again. All the same, it is tempting to accept the
interpretation of a long, empty month with no news,
no events or visits, no occupation but embroidery and
being read to, and weather so uncertain (as October in
Westmorland can sometimes be) that it was worth noting
when it was fine enough to make an afternoon excursion
to Whinfell.

On the first morning of November she got up betimes
and 'went up to the Pagan Tower to say my prayers

and saw the sun rise'. Here, for a moment, the narrative
of the diary can be related to a precise location in the
fabric of the castle as it stands today. Her bedroom in
the Gatehouse, the scene of her father's birth, her mother's
death and ultimately her own, is no more than a floorless,
roofless ruin, but one can still climb the spiral staircases
of the great stone Keep, into which it opened, and go one
storey higher to stand in the little oratory set in the
thickness of the north-eastern buttress. This top storey
was added to the earlier Norman building by the first
of the Cliffords in the 13th century, and looking up
and to the left, as one approaches the castle from
without, one can see the change in the stonework at this
corner, and the window from which his lonely descendant
got her first sight of the November sun.

The routine of reading and embroidery still went on.
At first sight there seems no particular reason for the
diarist to record that 'Upon the 4th I sat in the Drawing
Chamber all the day at my work', until we consider the
marginal note that accompanies it. It records that on
that day 'Prince Charles was created Prince of *Wales* in
the Great Hall at *Whitehall* where he had been created
Duke of *York* about 13 years before. There was banners
(has the copyist misread a word that should denote the
entertainment of fighting at *barriers*?) and running at the
Ring, but it was not half so great a pomp as was at the
creation of Prince *Henry*'. Obviously it had been an
important and enjoyable function. As there was running
at the ring, Lord Dorset was naturally chosen to take
part in it, and his young Countess might well have been
expected to be present. After all, it was not so very long
since she herself had danced at such functions, both before
and after her marriage, with Jonson or her old tutor
Daniel to devise the entertainment and Inigo Jones to
design her dresses and elaborate tires to set off her
beautiful hair. There is just the least savour of sour grapes
in the reflection that it was 'not half so great a pomp' as
the one in which she had played the nymph of Aire.
The entry goes on with a note of recent advancements

in the peerage and changes in official appointments, and reminds us that the discussion of such matters had been an integral part of the social life she had enjoyed. John Chamberlain's correspondence is full of it, and it is just such a life of miscellaneous interest in other people's affairs that King Lear imagines as lying before himself and Cordelia when they are led off to prison. It was the very spirit of the time and company in which she had spent her youth, and now, not unnaturally, she missed it.

Reading and needlework were beginning to pall. On the 9th she sat at her work and heard the faithful Rivers and Marsh read the Essays of Montaigne 'which book they have read almost this fortnight', and three days later she finished her cushion of Irish stitch, admitting that 'to pass away the time at work' had been her chief help in her present situation. A week later, however, there came a sudden change. William Punn, her overseer, arrived from London with letters from Lord Dorset that conveyed really surprising news. He had actually challenged Lord Clifford to a duel; the fact had become known, both of them had been summoned before the Privy Council and the King himself had acted as a mediator, reconciling the contestants and ordering Lord Dorset to send for his wife, so that the matter at issue might be considered and decided by his own royal judgement.

This, as Lady Anne naïvely admits, was a thing she had little expected, and at this point the entries in the diary change, and indicate a change of mind behind them. The day after the news came, she spent most of the day playing backgammon, and noted that all the time since her husband went away she had worn her black taffeta nightgown (something between a dressing-gown and a house-coat) and a yellow waistcoat, and used to get up early and walk on the leads before the day's reading. Now, it seems, she felt more like amusing herself, and started thinking about her clothes. She strung her mother's legacy of loose pearls and diamonds into a necklace. She called on a neighbour at Blencowe, listened to some music and went over the house and gardens. She heard, with regret, of impending quarrels between her husband's supporters and her cousin's, but there was nothing she could do about it, and she went on with her preparations, buying a warm cloak and a 'saveguard' (what Chaucer calls a foot-mantle) against the impending journey. Four of her servants, including the caterer and one whom she describes as 'Tom Fool' had been sent on ahead, and in the first week in December Peter Baskett arrived with the horses. The coach was not with them, having been left behind at Rose, 20 miles to the north. This little detail indicates that winter had really set in, and that many of the roads were, or might be, rendered impassable by snow. The route by Kendal and Shap was—and is—mountainous and difficult at the best of times, and not to be rashly attempted with the heavy coaches of 1616; the route by Appleby and Brough would be blocked as it climbed up into the drifts of Stainmore, and the only thing to do was to start off in the opposite direction as far as Carlisle, make the easier crossing to Newcastle and so reach the main . road to York and eventually to London. She was mounted on Rivers' mare (was this, one wonders, the horse that had fallen off the bridge in that earlier journey in March?) and notes with satisfaction that she covered 27 miles that day. It was a minor calamity that she mislaid a diamond ring when pausing at Rose Castle, but three days later William Punn, who had been left behind to look for it, overtook the party and Lady Anne had her ring again.

The journey to London took 10 days in all. When she got to Islington her husband was there to meet her, in a borrowed coach, and was attended by a number of friends, so that it was a procession of some 10 or 11 coaches that covered the final stage of the journey. Dorset House was 'well dressed up' for her arrival, and to crown her happiness her little daughter, whom she had not seen for 11 months, was brought down to meet her in the gallery. Whatever the future might hold, life at the moment seemed to be at its best again.

It continued to be enjoyable, and for a little while, at any rate, she was happier than she had been since her mother died. Two days before Christmas she had a new wrought taffeta gown, made for her by Lady St. John's tailor, and Lady Manners came in the morning to do her hair for her in the newest fashion in readiness for a function that evening at Northampton House. She and her husband went there in the family's state coach and took the child with them, to show her to their hosts, Lord and Lady Suffolk, Dorset's uncle and aunt, and parents of the imprisoned Lady Somerset. To her mother's delight, the child was a success. 'All the company commended her', and she was taken downstairs to be inspected and kissed by Lord Clifford, though Lady Anne tactfully stayed in company with Lady Suffolk and avoided what might have been an awkward meeting.

The suit for the estate was by this time a matter for much fashionable discussion and conjecture. It involved several great families, including the Howards, whose fortunes and standing at Court were themselves under-going remarkable fluctuations; it concerned vaguely mysterious and far-off castles in the north, and there was nothing embarrassing or unsavoury about it. Dorset was a well-known figure in the best sporting circles, his wife was neither unpresentable nor a shrew, but on the contrary a popular little person with a delightful baby, and—which carried the most weight of all—the King was now taking an active interest in the whole affair. Lady Anne sums up the position at this time in a tone of quiet contentment.

> All this time of my being at *London* I was much sent to, and visited by many, being unexpected that ever matters should have gone so well with me and my Lord, everybody persuading me to hear and make an end. Since the King had taken the matter in hand so as now.

It looks as if they had had a very happy Christmas.

On the day after Boxing Day she dined at Somerset
House with Lady Elizabeth Grey. Lady Compton and
Lady Fielding were there, and they all discussed her
impending interview with the King. Just after dinner
Lord Dorset joined them, and they all went to Arundel
House and saw the famous Arundel collection of pictures
and classical statuary. New clothes, friendly visits, parties,
and sight-seeing must have been doubly enjoyable after
the sad weeks that had gone before. On the 28th she
dined quietly upstairs because she was not very well—
apparently the Christmas hospitality was taking its toll—
but she was well enough in the afternoon to receive a
visit from her hostess of the day before and lose some
£27 to her at cards. On the last day of the year she sent
off one or two New Year gifts, including a 'sweet bag' to
the Queen, and the year 1616 came to an end rather
more happily than it had begun.

Chapter Six

THE JUDGEMENT OF KING JAMES
Put your main cause into the king's protection
Henry VIII, III, i

THE NEWS OF THE KING'S interest and proposed
intervention gave an extra spice to Court life in the
opening weeks of the new year, and Lady Anne's
existence now offered a complete contrast to those long,
empty days of the late 'back end', with their routine of
household embroidery, readings from improving books and
lonely walks upon the leads at Brougham. On New Year's
Day itself she went to see Lady Carey at the Savoy, and
on from there to wait upon the Queen at Somerset House,
where she saw various old friends, not to mention 'a
great deal of company that came along with the King
and the Prince'. Both King and Queen kissed her, and
Lady Arundel, her hostess at the last Twelfth-night
masque, had a long talk with her and urged her to follow
the King's ruling in the case, whatever it might be. From
there she went on to Essex House to see Lady Northumberland, and paid one or two more calls that day before and
after supper, and next day she paid a less fashionable
visit, going to see Lord and Lady Somerset in the Tower.
Reprieved from the gallows, to which they had both
been condemned, they were living an uneasy existence,
imprisoned and discredited, in the company of the
Earl of Northumberland, who had been in there for years,
on the suspicion, unproven and almost certainly un-
justified, of complicity in the Gunpowder Plot of 1605.

There was a certain distinction about being imprisoned
for treason—which could be regarded as a matter of
opinion, not a direct felony like murder—and Northumberland had come to reasonable terms with his position,
treating the place very much as if he owned it, ordering

his affairs from there and having one of his daughters to stay with him so that he could keep his eye upon her and prevent what he considered to be an unprofitable marriage. The Somersets made some attempt to emulate this attitude, going about with him as much as possible, but it was not altogether successful. Unproved treason was one thing, self-confessed instigation to murder was very much another, and though Somerset showed himself at a window now and then, and made a point of ostentatiously wearing his insignia as a Knight of the Garter, it did not arouse the favourable comment he had obviously hoped for. Lady Somerset, too, had little or no success with her attempts to be bright and popular. They only served to increase the general impression that she was quite unrepentant and not very respectable. Still, she was a Howard, and Lady Anne's cousin by marriage, and had a little child, and the Dorsets were not the kind to forsake their kinfolk in their adversity, even when some might have thought it advisable for them to do so. Lady Anne, at any rate, had not seen them since before the scandal broke, as she had been at Brougham when Lady Somerset was arrested and at Knole when she had been tried. Now that she was in London again, she was naturally calling on as many of her friends as possible, and the visit was a clear indication that she still counted the Somersets among their number.

Court favour was turning away, at this time, from the Howards and their kinsfolk, and directing its light upon another object. George Villiers, the King's current favourite, had already been given the Garter and raised to the peerage as Lord Whaddon and Viscount Villiers, now he was taken a step further and created Earl of Buckingham. Dorset was one of the supporting earls who brought him before the King for the formal ceremony of creation and investiture—a duty which he probably resented horribly—and Lady Anne had supper with her Howard cousins the Arundels and saw Fletcher's play *The Mad Lover* acted in the Hall. She gives no indication of her reactions to that far-fetched and extravagant piece. It is clear from the text that it was written to suit the powers of a leading actor who was no longer young but still possessed a good stage presence and the ability to move his hearers by reflective and poetic speeches reminiscent of Hamlet or of Cleopatra's Antony. Burbage, who had played both those parts and is known to have played this one, was in his 50th year, but it is not hard to imagine that with his personality, technique and experience to animate it, the frigid story might have come to life and been not only plausible but successful. The next night was Twelfth-night, and was celebrated in the more usual way—a visit to court, a 'scrambling supper' with Lady Arundel and Lady Pembroke, and standing-room after-wards in someone else's box to see the Twelfth-night masque. It was Ben Jonson's robust and jovial *Masque of Christmas,* and must have come as a lively contrast to the reflections, dead-marches and fantastic self-sacrifice of the night before.

The 'twelve days of Christmas' and their accompanying festivities brought their customary reaction in due course. When Twelfth-night was over, the Dorsets went down to Knole. Dorset was smarting under the thought of the triumphant Buckingham; his lady, suddenly caught up again in the whirl of Court life after her months of country solitude, was over-tired and over-excited, like a child who had had too many parties and late nights, and as an almost inevitable result, they fell out again over the question of the land. Next day the Earl sat sulking and reading in his study, while Lady Anne set things to rights in her own quarters and began to have a new book read to her—not a classical or devotional work this time but a recently-published volume of travels in Greece, Turkey, Egypt, Asia Minor and the Holy Land, written by George Sandys, a poet, scholar and translator of the classics. He had visited these regions in 1611 and on his return had compiled an account not only of what he himself had seen there but of the history and administration of the Turkish Empire, under which they were all governed. The book is a lively blend of personal narrative, explanation

and description, interspersed with scraps of very pleasant
verse, and would be a great and probably acceptable
change from the *History of the Netherlands* and the
Essays of Montaigne.

Dorset's day of isolation and study was followed
by abrupt and characteristic action. He went up to
London without telling his wife that he was going, or
what he meant to do there, and it was only in the
afternoon that she learned that he had gone. The
matter of the inheritance was to be brought to a head,
and in less than a week she got a peremptory summons
to come up to London next day, as she was to appear
before the King on the following Monday. She obeyed,
and went up on Friday the 17th, with the prospect of a
week-end in which to prepare herself, but on arrival
she learned that the King wanted to see her at once,
and an audience had been fixed for that very Saturday
afternoon. There was to be no time for her to collect
her thoughts and marshal her mother's reasoned arguments
or the evidence that supported them; there had been an
appeal to Caesar, and before Caesar she was to go.

There was, however, one chance that she could take,
and in her extremity she took it. Immediately after
dinner she had an audience with the Queen, to whom
Lady Derby explained the present position. Anne of
Denmark was essentially a kindly woman. Frivolous and
shallow as she was, there was a strain of shrewdness in
her, and she gave the unfortunate Anne a piece of
advice that was discouraging on the face of it, but
obviously sincere, and, as it turned out, useful. In the
Knole diary it is recorded that 'she promised me she
would do all the good in it she could'—which is as far
as princes' promises may go, and meant no more and
no less than politicians' promises today—but a marginal
note by Lady Anne is far more candid and expressive.
'The Queen gave me warning not to trust my matters
absolutely to the King lest he should deceive me'. That
counsel, unpalatable as it was, at least gave her an
indication of the best course to pursue, and that, in her

present position, was something to be glad of, even though it might seem no more than a counsel of despair.

She was soon to find out what good advice it was, and by how narrow a margin of time she had obtained it. Her audience with the Queen was cut short, or immediately followed, by a summons to accompany her Lord before the King. An unpalatable feature, at the very outset, was the fact that the intermediary who brought them into the royal presence was the detested and recently-ennobled Buckingham. The audience itself was private, and its object was very soon evident. Husband and wife knelt formally at either side of their King's chair while he urged them earnestly to be reconciled with each other and to entrust the whole matter to his kingly and fatherly judgement. King James always fancied himself as the British Solomon, and the thought of himself as a kind and gracious prince, condescending, in his divinely-inspired wisdom, to settle the affairs of his less fortunate subjects, would appeal to him tremendously. It would ease matters all round, and reflect great credit on him personally, if he could announce, at the formal meeting on Monday, that the parties were already in accord and prepared to accept his ruling on the legal position.

Naturally enough, Dorset fell in with this arrangement. He had a pretty good idea what that ruling would be, and knew that a 'composition' with the Cliffords would save him a lot of trouble and bring in some ready money, but Lady Anne was now upheld not only by her own wishes and convictions, but by the quite unrepeatable warning she had had from the Queen. From her account it looks as if the question of the lands was not officially the main point at issue until she introduced it herself, to the general embarrassment. Ostensibly, all they were being asked to do was to show their trust in their sovereign by expressing readiness to put the whole matter in his hands in the certainty of obtaining a just decision. On the face of it, a loyal subject could hardly do less, and a refusal could look very awkward indeed. It was a dilemma that had faced more than one loyal

subject in the past, and had been known to end fatally
with an accusation or even a formal charge of treason.
Archbishop Thomas of Canterbury had affirmed his
loyalty to Henry II 'saving God's honour and the rights
of Holy Church', and had been struck down and martyred
in his own cathedral. Thomas More had acknowledged
the supremacy of Henry VIII with reservations which
brought him to the scaffold and the axe. This case was
not one that affected the royal person or prerogative,
but a refusal might be taken personally as a reflection
on his honesty or his intelligence—as indeed it was.
All the same, Lady Anne was convinced of the justice
of her contention and was not prepared to abandon it.
Avoiding anything like open defiance of authority, she
made at the outset one respectful stipulation that made
havoc of the King's design. 'I beseech'd His Majesty to
pardon me for that I would never part from *Westmorland*
while I lived upon any condition whatsoever'.

That was her resolution, and she clung to it. King
James tried cajoling, he tried arguing, he seems to
have tried downright threatening and bullying, but she
was not to be moved. There was no hope of getting the
matter settled in private and avoiding arguments in
next week's hearing, and the audience ended in an
impasse, with the King obviously in a very bad temper.

Lord Dorset, on the other hand, was not. Though the
discussion had not availed his own interests, he did not
like the King's manners, and could not help admiring
the way Anne stood up to them. However badly he
himself might behave to his wife, that did not give
anyone else—not even the King of England—the right to
do the same. Moreover, her steadfastness in maintaining
her contention, in the face of royal bullying or blandish-
ment, made it clear, as nothing else could have done,
that there was nothing personal about it, no question of
her making it a pretext for quarrelling with himself.
It was a case of honest conviction, and she was clearly
prepared to maintain it before all the world, so he
admired her for it and was quite unexpectedly kind.

Lord and Lady Dorset went back to the Queen's apartment, picked up Lady St. John and saw her home, and then went home themselves. Next day, being Sunday, they went together to the Chapel Royal to attend the Queen—who did not, after all, come out that morning—after which Lady Anne dined with one of the Lady Ruthvens and was subjected to further advice from a number of fashionable friends, all urging her to put the matter into the King's hands. The Twelfth-night masque was repeated that evening, but she did not stay for it. She had seen it already, she had had an exhausting interview the day before and there was probably a still more exhausting one to come on Monday, and she can have been in no humour to enjoy the sallies of Father Christmas and his satellites—a comic Cupid not too sure of his lines, and his mother, Venus, deaf and officious, continually interrupting and fussing over the performance of her little boy. Lord Dorset came for his wife at six o'clock and Lady St. John gave them a lift home. It had not been a restful week-end, and Monday's ordeal was now very near.

At last, at eight o'clock in the evening, it came. They had gone to the Court immediately after dinner, Lady Anne to the apartment of her cousin by marriage, Lady Bedford, and her husband to the King to see to the final arrangements. Presently she was summoned to the King's Drawing-chamber as before, but this time to stand face to face with her opponents. Her uncle Cumberland and her cousin Clifford were there, as might be expected; so was the great Lord Arundel, one of the most distinguished of the Howards, so, also were their political adversaries that 'Incomparable Pair of Brethren', the Earls of Pembroke and Montgomery—the latter of them a former favourite of King James—and Sir John Digby, the Vice-Chamberlain. The Law was represented by the Lord Chief Justice, the Attorney-General and Sir Randal Crewe, Counsel for Lord and Lady Dorset. As things stood now, Lord Dorset's own position was an equivocal one. He was making formal

claim for the Westmorland property on behalf of his
wife. If, by any slender chance, that claim should succeed,
he would get the whole of it. If, on the other hand, it
should go to the Cliffords, he might get a substantial
honorarium (everybody would be too polite or tactful
to call it a bribe) so long as he had made things reasonably
easy for them, and not put too many obstacles in their
way. The odds were in favour of the latter course, but
there was still a gambler's chance of the bigger prize,
and Dorset was a gambler above all things. Direct
opposition at the outset, however, would get him
nowhere, so he agreed, as before, to leave the final
decision to the King. Perhaps, in spite of his wife's
obstinacy, the royal mind might be impressed by their
own lawyer's arguments after all.

The Cliffords declared their readiness to accept the
royal judgement, but Lady Anne stipulated, as before,
that she 'would never agree to it without Westmorland'.
Pembroke and the Attorney-General strongly opposed
her, but she was resolute, matters were at a deadlock,
and the King, in her own words, 'grew in a great chaff'.
(It is perhaps interesting to note that the expression 'fair
chuffed', or 'in a great chuff', is still used in Westmorland
at the present day.) The person who resolved the
situation was Lord Dorset. He saw the King's temper
rising, and guessed that he was on the point of forgetting
himself before them all, and going further, in his anger,
than he had done on Saturday in private. Whatever
happened, Dorset was not going to have his wife insulted,
particularly by someone whom he could not challenge
for it, and he roundly asked Digby to open the door
and let Lady Anne out. The Vice-Chamberlain obeyed,
and went out with her, making another unsuccessful effort
to get her to change her mind. More welcome, perhaps,
were the enquiries of Lord Hay, an old friend of the
King, but also a frequent visitor to Lady Anne's aunt
Bedford. The Court in general would be highly interested
in the situation, but would be chary of showing undue
attention or sympathy to someone who had come out so

suddenly from that session in the Drawing-chamber while they were still unsure what was going on inside. Lord Hay, on the other hand, with his reputation for fastidiousness, his notorious extravagance and his easy familiarity with the King, was not one to depend anxiously on the favour of princes or to shrink from the risk of being seen talking to the wrong people. Lady Anne might or might not be in danger or disgrace; what was evident was that she was in distress, and he came over to her, and, instead of lecturing her, listened while she told him briefly what it was all about. Nothing could have served better to calm down her passions and relieve her immediate fears. Interest and attention can do much to restore one's mental balance when indignant sympathy will only disturb it the more.

Then Lord Dorset came out and told her the result of the deliberations. Since there was no reasoning with her, the matter would be discussed and ultimately decided without her, and she would have to accept the agreement when it came, whatever its terms might be. To some this might seem like total defeat, but not to her. That they were stronger than she, she had never questioned. They could arbitrarily over-ride her will and her convictions, and now it seemed that they were going to do so. But—and this was of paramount importance to her—they could never say that she had approved of it, or agreed to it, or even passively accepted it. All the arguments and quarrels, all the flattery and cajolery, all the lectures, threats, browbeating and petty persecution had gone to show how much that acceptance meant to them, and at the end they had had to do without it, because she would not yield to their arguments and say they were right when she still firmly believed not only that they were wrong, but that they knew it. A very trying week-end was over, and she went down to Knole with a sense of relief.

One unexpected pleasure had been vouchsafed her, in that at the last moment, when the combined forces of the King, the lawyers and the Cliffords might have

been too much for her, her husband had come down
resolutely in her support, and had dared to have her
withdrawn from the meeting without consulting the
wishes of the King. Feelingly she ended her account of
the day, in the Knole manuscript, with the admission 'I
may say I was led miraculously by God's Providence,
and next to that I trust all my good to the worth and
nobleness of my Lord's disposition, for neither I nor
anybody else thought I should have passed over this
day as well as I have done'. That, at any rate, was
something to be thankful for, and she freely admitted
her thankfulness.

From grateful consideration of her husband, her thoughts
and cares turned towards her child. The day after her
return to Knole, the two-year-old Lady Margaret had
an attack of what seems to have been convulsions,
though her mother describes it loosely as 'her 6th fit
of the ague'. The coach was going up to London that
day, so she sent with it a letter to her husband telling
him of the child's illness, and at the same time thanking
him for his 'noble usage' of herself in her recent ordeal.
Dorset was genuinely attached to his little daughter,
and came down at once to see her, even though it
meant rising early next day and hurrying back to
London and Whitehall. The child was getting better,
and was put into a red baize coat instead of her baby-
clothes, which were given away, not long afterwards, to
Mr. Legge, the steward, whose wife was presumably in the
family way. Life settled down again into the old routine
of needlework and reading, punctuated by journeys
upstairs to see how the child was getting on. There was
no point in dressing very formally or elaborately when
there was hardly anyone to see how she looked, so she
went about in a plain green flannel gown made for her
by her overseer William Punn, and a 'waistcoat' (a
sleeved bodice without skirts to it) of yellow taffeta. At
the end of the month she had a visit from the Reverend
Jeffrey Amherst, rector of Horsmonden, who told her
the latest gossip from London, and it was distinctly

encouraging to hear. People were now saying that she had done well not to entrust her cause to the King 'and that everybody said God had a hand in it'. So, under God, had the Queen, but that was not generally known. At any rate, Lady Anne could not feel entirely friendless in her difficulties.

It was her husband, now, who was in need of all his faculties if he were to come out of the matter with any success. He had stood up for his lady on a point not of law, but of common courtesy and good breeding, and in so doing had not only opposed, but might even be thought to have criticised, the conduct of his King. Back-biters could very readily seize on this, if they were to hear of it, and magnify it into a case of rebellion against the Lord's Anointed, and he would have, accordingly, to be careful how he went. His tactics were simple, ingenious and successful. He kept in the public eye as much as possible—even the news of his little daughter's illness was not allowed to keep him away for long—and he was continually entering his birds against the King's in the cockpit at Whitehall. It cost a good deal of money, because by merit on their own part or careful selection on Dorset's the King's birds usually seemed to be winning, but its results were all that could be desired. James was delighted with him, was always being seen walking with him or heard speaking of him, and had him at his side, leaning on his very chair, when he treated the Star Chamber Court to a royal discourse on the evils of duelling. When the lawyers met again to consider the great inheritance question, the King was present at several of their meetings, indicating his sympathy, if not his impartiality, by his asseveration that there must be a law *somewhere*, if they could only find it, to disallow this troublesome Lady Dorset's claim.

Meanwhile, her opponents were ready and able to incense her husband against her in her absence. He wrote a letter indicating that he was displeased with her, and a visitor from London went down to Knole apparently for the purpose of telling her that her attitude was not at all well thought of by society in general. It was just the opposite of what she had heard from Dr. Amherst, and she could not really tell which to believe, so she turned to her only sure remedy and fell to her prayers. The child had another fit, which made her mother really anxious for her life, but a sudden nose-bleeding that same evening gave her unexpected relief. Rivers came down from London with the news that the case was still dragging on. It was supposed to be decided, but the award had not yet been officially announced. One comforting piece of news was that Lord William Howard was apparently dissatisfied with the decision. Lady Anne had always questioned her mother's mistrust of him, and had considered him to be firmly ranged against her adversaries. Then, much to her disappointment, he had taken their part for a time, but now, it seemed, the opposition was breaking up. Certainly he was not in such complete agreement with her husband as he had been before, and all might yet be well.

February dragged on, with little to vary the accustomed routine. Lord Dorset came down for one night, in the middle of the month, with an account of the state of the case, and of general doings at Court, and a letter from Lady Grantham brought an amount of general news from London. The child had another attack, and was given 'a salt powder to put in her beer'. Lady Compton, Lord Dorset's sister, separated herself from her husband and tried to borrow £77, but was sent only £10 in cash. Otherwise it was the usual programme of working, walking, reading or being read to, and looking after the child.

At this point the diary refers to the great family chronicle which was being compiled under Lady Anne's direction and eventually written out in triplicate. It embodied the results of Lady Cumberland's tireless research into the history of the Clifford and Vipont estates, with biographies of their successive owners, copies of wills and charters, and any other documentary material that could possibly be considered relevant. Marsh was at work upon it at this time, and it had been brought up to 1607. The work had a threefold attraction now for Lady Anne, as it was at once a tribute to her mother, a valuable compendium of evidence in support of her own case, and a source of encouragement and consolation. Even now, when the King's influence was being thrown into the scale against her, it was some relief to 'compare things past with things present and read over the Chronicles'. That, and her religious faith, sustained her as the dark February days went by.

With the coming of March the child began to get better, and the curtains of her sick-room, which had been kept close for the past three or four weeks, were drawn up to let in the spring daylight. Lord Dorset was away at Buckhurst, occasionally sending for his horses and hounds from Knole, but though his lady sent a letter on one occasion begging him to look in at Knole on his way to London, there is no suggestion that he complied. Her days were obviously monotonous, her evenings were usually spent playing cards with the steward, and for mental exercise she studied the Pentateuch with the chaplain, a Dr. Rann or Rand. It was quite an event to find, on the 11th, that little Lady Margaret had cut two 'great teeth . . . so that in all she had now 18'. Teething seems to have been at the root of her recent trouble, because we now hear no more of those 'ague fits' that had caused her mother so much anxiety. Otherwise, however, life was getting almost unbearably dull, and Lady Anne took to going to bed at eight o'clock and not getting up till eight next morning. Her appearance, too, was beginning to need attention. Her green flannel gown was not really suitable for a great lady in mourning for her mother, and apparently aroused some comment, for on the 14th of the month she made some effort to pull herself together, putting on her mourning gown of black grogram and intending 'to wear it till my mourning time is out because I was found fault with for wearing such ill clothes'.

That same afternoon, Peter Baskett arrived with news from London. The great meeting had taken place. Lord Cumberland and Lord Clifford had come to Dorset House, and the agreement with her husband had been signed and sealed that morning. The ancient entail had been ignored, the irregularity of her father's bequest had been dis-regarded, the Cliffords had long been in possession of her own birthplace at Skipton, and now her mother's jointure was gone too. For one summer and autumn she had been Lady of Brougham, riding round her estates and breathing the pure, keen air of the fells; now that in its turn was taken from her, and for all she knew, she might never see Westmorland again.

The signing of the agreement coincided with the King's departure for Scotland. It was the end of the winter season at Court, and Dorset had no longer any cause to stay there. He came down into the country, but not to Knole. The servants were sent down there, but he himself went to Buckhurst, and sent for Josiah Cooper, a French page, to wait on him, and for one of the cooks to make his broth, for at that time he was a very sick man, and had to break his journey once or twice on the way down, and take a rest. Lady Anne wrote at once, on hearing of his illness, asking permission to join him at Buckhurst, but it was not granted, and she had still to continue her lonely routine of prayer, cards, Bible-reading and embroidery. He joined her at Knole after some 10 days, and stayed there for a time, having let Dorset House to Francis Bacon. The Lord Chancellor, Sir Thomas Egerton, had just died, and Bacon, who had succeeded him as Lord Keeper of the Seals, needed a town house at short notice until such time as Egerton's official residence at York House—once his own birthplace— should be vacated and made ready for him. It was no more than a temporary arrangement, but it was a chance of ready money for Dorset, and would be very welcome in consequence.

On his first coming to Knole he was still far from well, being troubled with a cough, so that he did not

George Clifford, Earl of Cumberland, armed as Queen's Champion, about 1590. Miniature by Nicholas Hilliard. By courtesy of the National Maritime Museum.

He wears a pageant surcoat and hat, with the Queen's glove mounted as a cockade, and the armour of Greenwich make, decorated with golden stars, that appears in several portraits and seems to have been split up under the terms of Lady Anne's Will.

Pendragon Castle, Mallerstang. Burned by the Scots and rebuilt by Lady Anne, it was not maintained by her descendants, and bears out Camden's description of it as having 'nothing left unto it unconsumed by time, besides the bare name, and an heape of stones'.

*Costume design by Inigo Jones, for Lady Anne
to wear as Berenice of Egypt in Ben Jonson's* Masque
of Queens *at Whitehall in February 1609. Devonshire
Collection, Chatsworth. Reproduced by permission of
the Trustees of the Chatsworth Settlement.*

*Margaret, Countess of Cumberland. Painting on panel,
by Mark Gheeraerts, about 1600. Private collection.*

Richard Sackville, Earl of Dorset, Lady Anne's first husband. Miniature by Isaac Oliver, in the Victoria and Albert Museum.

The absence of leg-armour, and the fantastically elaborate plumes of the helmet on the table, indicate that he is preparing for a display of 'fighting at barriers', the fashionable combat on foot, across a waist-high partition, that had succeeded the mounted assaults-at-arms of the previous generation.

Lady Anne as Countess of Dorset, about 1615–1616. Portrait by William Larkin, long preserved at Knole but only recently identified as representing Lady Anne.

The style of her ruffles at neck and wrists is old-fashioned for its time, and strongly resembles that favoured by her mother. It was only in May and June 1617 that she began to dress her hair over a roll without a wire, and to have her gowns made 'with open ruffs after the French fashion'. Reproduced by courtesy of Lord Sackville.

Oratory in the Keep of Brougham Castle, where Lady Anne 'went up to the Pagan Tower to my prayers and saw the sun rise'. Reproduced by courtesy of the Society of Antiquaries.

Lady Anne as Countess of Pembroke, with her second husband, Philip Herbert, Earl of Pembroke and Montgomery. Detail from the great family portrait by Van Dyck, in the Double Cube room at Wilton. By courtesy of the Wilton Estate.

Lady Anne in her 'teens. Left wing of the triptych painted in 1645, probably by Jan Van Belcamp, and now in Appleby Castle.

This purports to represent Lady Anne at the age of 15, when in her own opinion she inherited her father's estates. The head resembles a miniature of her at about that age, but the dress is some 10 or 12 years later in style, and may represent an actual gown of hers still available at Baynard's Castle at the time of the painting.

Lady Anne at fifty-three. Right wing of the Belcamp triptych at Carlisle, representing her at the time of her actual coming into her inheritance.

Several head-and-shoulders versions of this, or studies for it, exist, having been given by her in old age to various friends. The expression of weary disillusionment may have expressed her feelings at the time, when it might well seem that she had attained her rights too late to have any hope of deriving enjoyment from them; but in fact she was to have more than 30 years of active and congenial life in the lands of her forefathers, and particularly in the Westmorland property that had been her mother's jointure.

Lady Anne's parents and brothers. Centre panel of the Belcamp triptych. The full-length figures are rather awkwardly worked up from head-and-shoulders pictures that would have been all the painter had to go on, but the labels and coats of arms running up each side trace the history of the Clifford family on one side and the Westmorland property on the other. All reproduced by the courtesy of The Lady Hothfield.

Period Costume, as imagined in the 17th century. Title-page designed by Jodocus Hondius for Speed's Theatre of Great Britain, *1611, and re-engraved by William Marshall for Sir Richard Baker's* Chronicle, *1643. It is even found, though very rare, in copies of the second edition, published four years after the King's execution.*

share his wife's bedroom, but 'was fain to lie in Leicester Chamber'. It seems, also, that he was not quite clear in his mind about the exact terms and implications of the royal award. He told her that the matter was not absolutely settled independently of her, but that there was provision made for agreement on her part; but it is significant that he found her reading Deuteronomy with Mr. Rann and said that she must leave off, or get someone else to read it with her, because 'it would hinder his study'. Dr. Williamson takes this as a reflection on the harsh quality of the chaplain's voice, for which there is no other evidence, but considering the size of Knole and the fact that Dorset was not sharing his wife's quarters at the time, it is hard to think that he would be unavoidably within earshot. A far more likely explanation is that he was confused by the complicated provisions of the document and wanted to puzzle them out with the assistance of the chaplain, in order to make quite sure what he was to get, and when, and on what terms. The important thing, from his point of view, was that the Cliffords were to pay him £20,000 in instalments, and that the time of the final payment would depend on his lady's agreement to the award and its ratification by Parliament. To ensure the Cliffords' quiet enjoyment of the property, the King ruled that if Lady Anne should survive her husband and start any further lawsuits about the estate, she should lose all her rights under her father's will, including the £15,000 in money that he had left her, and pay back the £20,000 to the Cliffords as well, or, in default of this, forfeit estates to the value of £25,000 which Dorset had put in pledge for the purpose. All this is complicated enough in itself, but is still more so in the legal language of the award, and it is not unnatural that Dorset felt that his chaplain—the professional scholar on the household staff—would be better employed in going through it with him than in reading to his wife about the sanitary regulations laid down for the Children of Israel in the Wilderness.

She finished reading Deuteronomy by herself, and next day she went walking with her husband in the garden and the park while he explained matters to her as well as he could. What upset her, it seems, was not so much the main award as the low opinion he seemed to have had of her, as implied by those elaborate precautions against her repudiating the agreement after his death. That really hurt, whereas the deprivation of her inheritance was merely a matter for indignation against her cousins. She and her husband were really fond of each other, which made it all the easier for them to hurt each other, and it was clear to her that these precautions had been imposed on him by the advice of Edward Lindsey, the business man who was receiver of his rents and had acted as agent in the matter of her mother's gold chain, and Matthew Caldicott, the 'favourite', whom she disliked and slightly feared because of his bad influence on her husband. Still, it meant that they had done something by antagonising Lord William Howard, who might turn out to be helpful to her after all.

So she sat indoors over her embroidery and did her best 'to sit as merry a face as I could upon a discontented heart'. Her attitude was well rewarded, because next day Lord Dorset had to go to London for a couple of nights or so, and on seeing him down to his coach she found that he was much better pleased and satisfied with the agreement than she had expected. The last days of March, when he had gone, she spent walking and sitting in the park, thinking matters over and finding, possibly to her own surprise, that she had a more contented mind than she had enjoyed for weeks. The injustice had been done, the King and the judges had given their ruling and it seemed that she must wait indefinitely for the chance of her inheritance or risk losing it altogether, but at least there was to be no more fighting. Her dear lord had got what he wanted, and was satisfied, and that made all the difference in the world.

Chapter Seven

AFTER THE AWARD

Mad world! mad kings! mad composition!
King John, II, i

ALL THE SAME, the matter was not yet concluded. A few days later, to her surprise, she learned that though there had been a general agreement, there had been no formal confirmation, but that the documents in the case had been lodged with Bacon and with Sir Henry Hobart, Chief Justice of the Common Pleas, to await the next law term for their final signing and sealing. Dorset came to her privately in her room and complained that there was much less money in her estate than the others had led him to believe. Soon he was back at his old technique of mixed cajolery and upbraiding, but she was used to that by now, doing all she could to assure him of her affection, but continuing in her resolve that she 'would never part with *Westmorland* upon any condition whatsoever'. Next day he sulked, and would not go to the nursery for his usual visit to his daughter, so her mother had the child brought down to them in her own room. The dissension did not last, however; a few days later they were together again, and Lady Anne was able to sit with her husband and brother-in-law and hear the latest news from Court, including the beginnings of a story about Lord Roos and his young step-grandmother the Countess of Exeter.

Neither husband nor wife was in very good health just then. Dorset was so ill one night, and unable to sleep, that Lady Anne moved out of their bed into a pallet, and next night she moved into the room of her attendant Judith Shrimpton, but though he was much better in a day or two, and was quite good company, she herself went down with a feverish cold. Nevertheless she was not too ill to work, and though she would not appear at meals she

sent for Marsh and spent the day drafting letters
to her former tenants in Westmorland about the altered
state of affairs.

It was now Holy Week. On Wednesday, 16 April
they had another discussion upon the old subject, but
she stood firm by her pledge to her mother and her
assurances to all the world that she would never renounce
her heritage, and on Maundy Thursday Dorset was
apparently so much impressed by her steadfastness that
he resolved never to trouble her with any more attempts
at persuasion. His resolution, however, was not so firmly
fixed as hers, and did not last much longer than Good
Friday. By the Saturday night he was urging her again,
still without success. She had signed 33 letters to
the Westmorland tenants, and Marsh had gone off with
them that day, and though she still would not agree to
the award in principle, she had accepted it in practice,
and had instructed them to do so, and accordingly felt
'in perfect charity with all the world', and in a proper
frame of mind to make her Easter Communion, which
she did next day in the company of her lord and most of
the household.

There was another quarrel that afternoon, apparently
due to mischief-making by Matthew Caldicott, but the
tone of the diary here takes a happier turn, with the
advance of spring and some apparent improvement in
Dorset's health and temper. We read of Lady Anne
wearing a white satin gown and white waistcoat, of
visits received and paid, including a special one to see
flowers in a neighbour's garden at Sevenoaks, and of
bouts of 'Burley-break', a game of the catch-as-catch-can
variety, on the bowling-green in the long, fine evenings.
Lord Dorset's attendant gentleman was his kinsman
Thomas Glenham, who had been with him on his various
journeys to London and the north and was evidently more
acceptable company, in Lady Anne's view, than the unpleasant Matthew. Dorset himself moved back into his
wife's room—after one false start, in which they 'fell out
about matters'—and it is clear that they were reconciled.

Quarrels and all, she was happier to have him in the house than to sit at home over her embroidery while he was amusing himself in London or in the hunting-field, or at the races at Lewes.

He was not a faithful husband. Aubrey says he had children by Lady Venetia Stanley, who was better known, later, as his brother's mistress until she married Sir Kenelm Digby, became a model of respectability, and was accepted everywhere. Possibly the children Aubrey mentions were the two natural daughters of Dorset's whom Lady Anne is reported to have brought up under her own care. One of them died in her minority, but Lady Anne arranged a marriage for the other with a clergyman named Belgrave, whom she presented to a living in Sussex. (A John Belgrave had at one time been a page at Knole, and Lord Dorset had left him an annuity of £20 in his will, whereas Cooper, the other page, got £200 down, so it may well be that Dorset was in fact making some slight provision for his unofficial son-in-law.) There was also a notorious woman-of-the-town called Bess Broughton, but entanglements of this sort were all—or nearly all—kept at a proper distance from his wife. Matthew was the only person to give her cause for complaint or jealousy under her own roof, and even that connection, objectionable as it was, counted for comparatively little against her husband's charm. He was barely 28, and she was 10 months younger, and they still found much in life to enjoy when they were together.

News from Brougham was depressing but not un-expected. Richard Dawson, an old servant of her mother's, came to report that Lord Cumberland's people had taken over the place, her own things had been stored in the Baron's Chamber in the castle, with one John Ruvy as caretaker, the plate had been sent to Lord William Howard's at Naworth for safe keeping, and her resident servants all dispersed. There was nothing to be done about it; she had written her letters and told the tenants what they were to expect and where their loyalties must

lie. Now she could only turn to her duties and occupations
near at hand, working at her everlasting embroidery, reading Chaucer and Sandys in her husband's company, and
seeing to the clothes and progress of the child. Lady
Margaret would be three years old on 2 July. Early
in the year she had been promoted to short-coats of red
baize, when her old baby-clothes were given to Mrs. Legge.
Three months later, at the end of April, she put on
a boned bodice for the first time—a foretaste of the
rigid Elizabethan and Jacobean corset that was to be
mercifully out of fashion by the time of her maturity.
With the beginning of May her mother cut away the
leading-strings from the shoulders of her red baize coats
and she began—after a few experimental tumbles—to
walk alone, being promoted next day to her first lace-
trimmed coat. She was out of babyhood now, and was
beginning her training as a young lady of quality.

Dorset went up to London at the beginning of May,
to take part in the new Lord Keeper's splendid procession from Dorset House to Westminster for the opening
of the new law term. Even in the King's absence in
Scotland it was still an elaborate function, the Queen
and Prince Charles both sending their followers to aug-
ment the train. Privy Councillors, judges and the nobility
in general turned out to do him honour, and Lord
Dorset had cause to be particularly assiduous. For one
thing, his own house was Bacon's present headquarters, and
for another, a new term was beginning and the great agreement with the Cliffords about the property, and their *ex
gratia* payment, was to be formally concluded on the 21st
of the month. Indeed, he was too busy to write to his
wife, who retaliated by leaving him in his turn without
a letter, and concentrating instead on doing her hair in a
new style, over a padded roll and not borne out by wires
after the former fashion. The weather grew hot, the child
was taken out of red baize and put into her white summer
clothes, and as the 21st drew nearer the steward came
from London with the usual news that Lord Dorset was
'much discontented' with his lady for not being more

accommodating, while Woolridge came from the north
to wait upon his mistress at Knole. There was nothing
more for him to do in Westmorland, as the property
had been handed over and the Cliffords had taken
possession as if everything were signed and sealed.

A few days later there came another anniversary, and
a sad one, since 24 May marked the day of Lady Cumberland's death. Her daughter spent it in arranging the
books which had arrived from Brougham and talking
about the old days with Woolridge, who seems to have
had the sad duty of supervising the removal of the dead
lady's personal property when the castle was being cleared
for its new occupants. But the past was past, and it was
necessary to cope with the affairs of the present and take
thought for those of the future. For one thing, it was
time to go out of mourning. However sad she felt, she
had no excuse now for abandonment to outward sorrow;
she must be seen to put a bold face on adversity, and one
of the ways of doing so was to get some new clothes.

On the 25th, she was measured for a new gown by
Lady St. John's tailor, the same who had made the
black taffeta dress she wore at Christmas, and this
may have softened the blow she felt that same afternoon,
when a letter from her cousin Russell told her that
Dorset had cancelled the generous jointure-settlement
he had made upon her in the preceding year. She resolved
to bear this patiently, and wrote to tell him so—though
she was naturally displeased—and she made a point of
writing friendly letters to his married sisters and to his
aunt, Lady Glenham. Now that she was out of retirement, it would not do to neglect her social responsibilities,
and she set out to make herself as pleasant as possible
to her husband's family. She was still in touch with his
cousin, Lady Somerset, the imprisoned murderess, who
had recently sent her a 'token'—she does not say what—
from the Tower by the hand of another cousin, Sir
Edward George.

The usual stray gossip was brought to her from one
source or another—that her cousin Clifford had been to

Brougham to look over the castle but had not slept there;
that the tenants in Westmorland still thought very kindly
of her and disliked their new landlords; that a good many
people blamed her for her obstinacy and, on the other
hand, that many commended her for her strict adherence
to what was just and honourable. She was not, apparently,
feeling very well. She mentions going 'into a bath' a
term denoting an elaborate operation of the Turkish-bath
variety, with hot stones and steam, and· a few days later
she went on a visit to one Goodwife Cicely and upset
herself by eating too much cheese. Her husband came
down to Knole for Whitsuntide, and they went to
church together, but she could hardly look up because
her eyes were 'so blubbered with weeping', and in the
afternoon they quarrelled again about Matthew. It did
not last, however; the fine June evening may well
have been too much for ill-temper on either side, and
once again they played barley-break* on the bowling-
green after supper.

All the same, the strain was getting almost too
much for her to bear. Presumably Dorset went back
to London next day; his departure, and her sudden
renewed isolation, may account for a drastic and unusual
move on her part. She wrote to the Bishop of London
complaining of Matthew Caldicott.

The diary does not indicate what she said, but she
must have been very near hysteria to have written at
all. To denounce his intimacy with Lord Dorset, or even
his influence over him, would imply a reflection on
her husband's morals, or at least his strength of character,
a piece of disloyalty which Lady Anne would usually be
at all pains to avoid, while a charge of mere mischief-
making would carry much less weight and might draw down
censure on herself for doing the same thing and bringing
the Bishop into it. We hear nothing more of the letter,
nor of any consequences arising from it. Possibly the

---

*The more usual spelling. Lady Anne's earlier 'Burley-break'
was one of her characteristic variations.

Bishop used his discretion and took no action in the matter; possibly Lady Anne changed her mind, having relieved her feelings by writing it, and it was never sent at all. At any rate, she got cheering news that same day from London, to the effect that her George and Russell cousins were doing all they could for her, and that the famous Award had not yet received the final confirmation of a grant under the Great Seal.

Meanwhile, the tailor from London was getting on with his work, and a few days later her new gowns were far enough advanced for her to have a fitting. She was at least sufficiently interested to mention the fact, and to note that one dress was of sea-green satin and the other of damask embroidered with gold, and that both were made 'with open ruffs after the French fashion' —that is, with the neck and breast bare, and the ruff standing up at the back and sides only, so as to form a background to the carriage of the head. It was a style much affected by the Queen, and gave much more freedom—especially at meal-times—than the great cart-wheel ruff, completely encircling the neck, that had preceded it and was still worn by old-fashioned people, or on formal occasions.

At the same time, it was clear that her friends were doing what they could for her in London. Woolridge brought her very favourable news from Court, which caused her to send back, by the way of the lady-in-waiting, a letter of gratitude to the Queen. Sir Edward George wrote to tell her how matters were going on, and what care Lord Francis Russell was taking of her interests, and enclosed a letter from Lady Somerset in the Tower. Her husband, who was away hunting, sent her 'an indifferent kind letter' and half a buck. Venison, however, was not to her taste, and she sent it on at once to Sir Edward George with her letter of thanks. After that, she relapsed into the old routine of working and walking 'as in many wearisome days besides'. She must have been in very low spirits to have any talk on the subject with her pages, but while gathering cherries in the

garden she talked with Josiah Cooper the French page,
who assured her of the affection of all the men in the
household—except, of course, Matthew 'and two or
three of his consorts'. It was not encouraging to have
Lord Dorset go up to London for a Howard christening.
That meant close association with Prince Charles and,
consequently, with his own brother, Edward Sackville,
whom she always suspected of intriguing to get all
the family property instead of little Lady Margaret,
who would otherwise be her father's heiress. She had
been served that way by her own father, and would
be very ready to suspect a repetition of the injustice.

Sure enough, a letter from Sir George Rivers told her
that her husband was indeed settling his lands upon his
brother, and she spent much of the next day in tears,
paying a visit to Withyam to see the tomb of her husband's
grandfather (that Lord Buckhurst who had been a main-
stay of Queen Elizabeth in her last days), and going
right down into the vault itself. She was ill, and wretched,
and almost broken in spirit, and when a messenger brought
her a kind letter from Lady Rich she took the opportunity
to give him a letter to take back to London to Lord
Dorset, appealing to him to come down and see her. A
pain in her side, 'which I took to be the spleen', kept
her indoors for the next two days, and to crown all,
Marsh brought down to her the text of the King's award,
sealed and made absolute at last.

In her opinion, it was as bad as it could be. Nevertheless,
there were certain things that would have to be done
about it, and ill as she was, she put them in hand.
A Mr. Davis, apparently her solicitor, came to Knole
and was instructed to prepare an abstract of it to be
sent down to the tenants. Fond of her as they were,
they must be given to understand what the law had
decided, and there must be no more opposition to
Lord Cumberland's people at hay-time, as there had
been the year before. It was bitter, and might seem
like capitulation on her part, but it was only fair to the
tenants that they should know the legal position at once.

In this extremity of depression her husband came to her 'he being something kinder to me than he was, out of pity in regard he saw me so much troubled', and it cannot have been very long before they realised that there was an independent reason for her continued sickness, her bouts of almost hysterical sorrow and complaint alternating with forced merriment and barley-break upon the green. Their springtime reconciliation had been a sincere one, and she was going to have another child.

The decision in regard to Westmorland seems to have aroused considerable interest among friends and neighbours in general. Lady Wotton had been in a hunting-party with Lord Dorset at Sir Percival Hart's castle at Lullingstone near by, and she rode to Knole to see Lady Anne and learn what she proposed to do about it. It was very natural that she should be interested, in view of that afternoon of silent companionship at Whitehall 18 months before, on the eve of the solemn family council at Dorset House when the Archbishop of Canterbury was brought to lecture poor Anne on her duty to her husband and cousins. Lady Wotton had spoken nothing of the matter then, 'though her heart and mine were full of it', and we cannot be sure whether her visit on this occasion was intended to reassure her cousin in her attitude or persuade her to submission. Whichever it may have been, she saw at once that persuasion would be fruitless and reassurance unnecessary, and she did not waste time on either, but 'stayed not above an hour in regard she saw I was so resolutely bent not to part with Westmorland'. Quite clearly she was a woman of discretion.

Inevitably, the whole position was intensified by the thought of the coming child. If it were a boy, then there would be no question of Dorset's settling his estate upon his brother. It would go on for another generation in the direct line, and Lady Margaret would take second place, but to a brother, not to an uncle or cousin as her mother had had to do. Meanwhile, the letters to the tenants were ready for signature, there were

one or two tokens to be sent to friends in the north—a
bent coin to one, a pair of gloves to another—and a
rather distinguished guest to be received. John Donne
had long been a brilliant and witty poet, place-hunter and
man-about-town, writing a passionate Eclogue on the
marriage of the Earl and Countess of Somerset and
attaching himself nevertheless to Somerset's adversary,
William Herbert, Earl of Pembroke. He had never
succeeded in getting a Court appointment of the kind
he desired, and now, in his 40s, he had decided to seek
a career in the Church. He had been ordained two
years by this time, was already a Doctor of Divinity,
and was ultimately to become Dean of St. Paul's. Lady
Anne went to church both morning and afternoon on
the following Sunday to hear him preach, and entertained
him to dinner afterwards, with other visitors, in the Great
Chamber. Each of them aroused, and retained, the other's
interest: Lady Anne, years later, included the published
volumes of his poems and his sermons in the books
painted in the background of her portrait, and he for
his part commented, as Bishop Rainbow records in her
funeral sermon, on her ability to talk intelligently on
apparently any subject from predestination to sleave-silk.
The phrase is no mere extravagance by a literary man;
her memories of keeping silkworms as a little girl, and her
religious reading as a lonely and neglected wife all had
their part in that lively, all-embracing mind, and were
available at need to illustrate appropriate points in
conversation.

Interesting and intelligent company like Donne's must
have been very welcome, for without it, and in her
husband's continued absence hunting, racing, or courting
other women, it is clear that she was desperately bored.
On the last day of July she 'sat still, thinking the time
to be very tedious', and it may well have been by a
sudden reaction against it that she rode next day to
Lullingstone in some state, with her cousin Moll Neville,
her attendant, Kate Burton, 'and as many horses as I
could get'. Lady Rich came down from London to meet

her there, and apparently brought her the latest gossip;
how Lord Roos had gone abroad on a diplomatic mission,
after having continued differences with his wife, and
there was some sort of trouble blowing up for a storm,
involving them and Lady Exeter. It had been noted
some time before the Dorset's younger brother, Edward
Sackville, ran a risk of being connected with it, but
matters had not yet come to a culmination.

Next day Dorset was back at Knole, and there was
another cause for disagreement. Bacon had at last moved
out of Dorset House and settled in his official residence,
the place needed setting in order and its owner wanted
his wife to see to it. She was not well, and far from
happy, and she refused point-blank, 'in regard things
went so ill with me'. Dorset's retort was to forbid her to
go with him to Penshurst on the following day, though
there was a house-party there for the hunting, and her
host and hostess had sent her a special invitation. His
argument would be that if she was not well enough to
undertake what he considered to be her housewifely
duties, she was not well enough to go riding abroad for
her own pleasure. Possibly he soon repented of what
might seem a rather petty retaliation, possibly, on the
other hand, he was right in his judgement and it would
not, at that time, have been good for her to go. At all
events, they parted on quite good terms, and when he
left he gave her a little present, a ring that had been
his grandmother's.

Preparations were in hand for him to go on a round
of visits among the neighbouring landowners for the
hunting, and the occasion was an important one, his
journey being made in considerable state and dignified
with the name of a Progress. In its way, it was an
English version of what King James had been doing
that summer, when he went up to his native Scotland,
re-visited after so many years, and came back by easy
stages, resting and being entertained in noblemen's houses
—including Brougham, where the triumphant Cliffords
provided a lavish musical programme for him with

singers and instrumentalists brought up at great expense from London. Dorset's own tour was less formal but almost as important in its neighbourhood and probably, for some of those concerned, almost as expensive. He could go away and enjoy himself with a free heart, since in view of his lady's approaching confinement nobody would expect her to be taking part in any such expedition, and there would be no need of explanation or apology for his leaving her in solitude at Knole. Their separation, for the next few months, would seem the most natural thing in the world.

There was one thing, however, that was likely to cause trouble independently of the inheritance, and that was Lady Anne's implacable dislike of Matthew Caldicott, her lord's confidant and officially-designated 'favourite'. We never hear his side of the matter, but the references in the Knole diary imply that she considered him to be instrumental in fostering difference between her husband and herself. There is a great difference between him and Dorset's cousin and other intimate companion, Tom Glenham, whom she rather liked. Matthew's equivocal position in Lord Dorset's affections gave him obvious opportunities for mischief-making, and she was convinced that he took full advantage of them. She made no secret of her feelings, and just before the start of the Progress the Chaplain, Mr. Rann, came to her and urged her to be more friendly to the man, but she replied that he had done her so many ill turns that she could not forget them. That week-end she was 'very troubled and sad in mind', and on the Monday, when the cavalcade set out from Buckhurst 'very gallant, brave and merry', Mr. Rann brought her a personal message from Matthew saying how much he would welcome her favour and good opinion. This was a gesture that could not be lightly disregarded, and she replied that 'as I was a Christian I would forgive him'. It was something very far short of friendship, which they must both have known to be neither possible nor particularly desirable, but at least they had patched up an uneasy peace.

This may have contributed to Lord Dorset's good spirits, for a week later he wrote her 'a very kind letter' from Lewes. She answered it at once, and then rode over to Penshurst to spend the afternoon and evening with the Lisles, where she saw a good deal of company, heard a good deal of news and enjoyed herself very much before returning home at night, with her cousin Barbara Sidney bearing her company for a good part of the way. After that life seems to have relapsed into its normal tedious routine and afforded nothing much to record in her diary. There was a rumour that her unpleasant brother-in-law, Edward Sackville, had been involved in a duel, and then news that he had been killed in it, but a few days later the Widow Duck came from London and said that there had been no such thing—probably to Lady Anne's secret disappointment. There was a visit that same afternoon from Sir Thomas and Lady Worth, whom she had met at Penshurst, and a fortnight later she made an excursion on horseback to visit Lady Selby at Ightham Mote, but otherwise it was a matter of sitting at home feeling none too well and hearing of her lord's 'merry progress far out of Sussex', which involved meeting the King at Woodstock, paying a visit to Bath and then going to London to collect the first instalment of the £20,000 due to him from the Cliffords. It was the first ready money he had received for the surrender of his wife's inheritance.

The diary records little for October. Sir Percival Hart came over from Lullingstone to dine, and a fortnight later Lady Lisle and Barbara Sidney came from Penshurst and talked of the Cliffords and other matters, but the summer was over, and both the season of the year and Lady Anne's condition restricted her to more static occupations indoors, such as making quince marmalade and re-stringing her jewels. In November she went up to London (apparently in the company of her brother-in-law and her cousin, Charles Howard, since her husband spent the time at Buckhurst and Lewes), saw some company, and went to Court. Fashions in costume had taken a welcome change, and the old drum-shaped farthingale was no longer *de rigeur,* so she was able to wear her new dress of embroidered green damask without its interior stiffening and support. She went to see Lady St. John, whose tailor had made it for her, and then went for the last time to the house that had been her mother's in Austin Friars, and the room in which she had been married nearly nine years before. It looked very different now, and she was moved to tears as she went from room to room, finding little or nothing of the pictures and furniture she remembered. Leaving that desolate house she went to Whitehall, to be comforted by the kindness of Lady Arundel, who was arranging for her to see the King next day.

The audience was an informal one. After 'an extreme great feast' in the company of her cousins she went to Whitehall and was summoned in due course to the Queen's bedchamber, where she found the King. He was at his most benign, kissed her and used her very graciously, telling her to go to his attorney and explain the position in detail, so that he himself could be thoroughly informed of her requirements. After all, he had got what he wanted; his decision had been signed, sealed and accepted, the Cliffords were established in Westmorland and had entertained him very well at Brougham, so he could afford to forget that other meeting, when he had so nearly lost his temper at being defied. There would be no harm done by giving this importunate little lady a chance to explain her grievances to someone else, and, after all, nothing could be done, or at any rate nothing *need* be done, to alter the arrangements now. She lost no time in complying, but went to Gray's Inn with Davis her agent on the following day, made her official application as instructed, called on a Mr. Walton (otherwise unidentified) for his advice and assistance, and returned home to Knole.

A note in her diary that 'the next day my Lord *Hay* was married to Lady *Lucy Percy*' has a more personal significance than at first appears. Lord Hay was the

courtier who had received Lady Anne's confidences, and
soothed her distress and anxiety, when she came out
from that stormy interview with the King in January,
and for some time he had been paying court to Lady
Lucy, daughter of the Earl of Northumberland, who had
for years been in enforced residence in the Tower on
account of his supposed connection with the Gunpowder
Plot. The great northern family of the Percies had a long
tradition of antagonism with their neighbours over the
Scottish borders, and Lord Hay was a Scotsman, a widower
and a person of a splendid and extravagant way of life,
all features which made him in Northumberland's eyes,
quite unsuitable as a son-in-law. Indeed, when Lady Lucy
had gone with her sister Lady Sidney to visit their father
in the Tower early in the year, he had commanded her
to stay with him, saying, according to Chamberlain, 'that
he was a Percy and could not endure that his daughter
should dance any Scottish jigs', but that he meant to
keep her under his own eye. Lady Sidney was told to
go back to her husband and arrange for her sister's maids to
be sent to wait on her in her new quarters. Northumberland's imprisonment was not rigorous, being rather a
kind of house arrest. He had more or less the run of
the place, and there was no objection to his having his
daughter to keep him company, so she duly remained
in residence there, and even had some kind of social
life, being allowed, and even encouraged, to visit the
notorious Lady Somerset every day. Northumberland
was himself supposed to be carrying on an intrigue with
this lady, and felt that this gave him good pretext for
his more frequent visits, but what he had not counted
on was the fact that Lord Hay was appointed independently to visit Lady Somerset on the King's behalf, and
was in a position to continue his courtship as much as
ever. Moreover, Lady Somerset actively encouraged the
match, and Northumberland found himself in worse
case than before. He sent his daughter away from the
Tower after all, but her mother was not prepared to
have her back, and she went to join her sister at Baynard's

Castle, and thence to the official residence of Lord Hay
as Master of the Wardrobe. Hay himself was by this
time away with the King in Scotland, but he had left
£2,000 for her maintenance until he should return for
the wedding. The fact that the King had promised to
attend, and to give away the bride, must have done much
to bring Lady Northumberland to a more tolerant frame
of mind, for by the summer she had her daughter living
with her at Sion, and Lord Hay was in and out of the
house every day, having rented a place near by, where
he gave feasts of such elaboration and splendour that
Lady Northumberland never dared to ask him to a meal
in return. Chamberlain's letters to Dudley Carleton are
full of the affair at its various states, and Lady Anne's
note of the marriage marks the culmination of something
with which her family had been connected, in one way or
another, from the very outset. The courtship had been
initiated with the help of her 'aunt Bedford', who had
acted as hostess for Hay at an official entertainment
(when Chamberlain had described her as 'Lady and
Mistress of the feast, as she is of the managing of his
love to the Earl of Northumberland's younger daughter'),
and had been assisted in the Tower by her husband's first
cousin. Indeed, the Bedford-Somerset connection was
to be kept up in the succeeding generation, for little
Anne Carr, the child born just before her mother's
imprisonment, was in time to become the bride of that
William Russell who in time became fifth Earl and first
Duke of Bedford. Lady Anne's Royalist sympathies
must have been disturbed, however, in later years by
the conduct of Lord Hay's own bride. He was advanced in
the peerage as time went on, to the Viscounty of Doncaster and the Earldom of Carlisle, and she was therefore
that Lady Carlisle who disclosed to John Pym and his
colleagues the intention of Charles I to come down personally to the House of Commons and arrest them—an action
which may be said to have led directly to the Civil War.

From Dorset's point of view, the first payment by
the Cliffords meant that the King's award was an

established fact, everything was happily concluded and no one need worry or argue the matter any more. Next time his lady was in London, he brought her cousin Clifford along to see her in what he imagined to be a friendly call. Clifford did not want to come, and Lady Anne, who was far from well, had no reason to want to see him, but Dorset brought him relentlessly into her bedroom 'where we talked of ordinary matters some quarter of an hour, and so he went away'. The experiment had not been a success, and the diarist was not going to pretend that it had been. Old Sir John Taylor, four days later, had a very different reception, as he spent two hours talking of the old days, of Lady Anne's father and the north. She had spent only six months in Westmorland at this time, but that was where her heart was, and already she knew it.

The year was drawing on to an end, and she might expect her child at the end of January. There was a momentary scare that little Lady Margaret might be sickening for smallpox, but it proved to be a false alarm. Dorset went off to Buckhurst, taking the greater part of the household with him, and held a sporting house-party there for three days, and after its breaking-up he stayed on for a week, with no company but the ubiquitous Matthew. Doubtless he found life dull at Knole, and for Lady Anne, lonely, ailing and disappointed, it was duller still. Everybody went up to London for Christmas at Great Dorset House. Lord and Lady Dorset dined 'below' —i.e., in state, not in the privacy of their rooms—and on the following Sunday Lady Anne went to church. Her two waiting-women were in their liveries, and she herself, while in no condition to wear the rigidly-boned or plated corset of the time, wore a rich night-gown (a coat-like garment, be it remembered, corresponding to the later dressing-gown) and petticoat. There was a dinner-party that night, and there, for a year, the Knole diary ends. There are no entries for 1618, but we know that at last, on 2 February, her son was born.

Chapter Eight

STANDSTILL

Who loses and who wins; who's in, who's out
King Lear, V, iii

THE DIARY ASSIGNS no reason for ·the complete blank between 28 December 1617 and New Year's Day 1619, but we may still be permitted, nonetheless, to account for it in the light of evidence in the text and from outside sources. For one thing, it is clear from the 1617 entries that Lady Anne's health at this time was not good. Her occasional reference to 'things going ill with her' need not be taken as referring exclusively to her difficulties with her husband or her claim to the Westmorland estates. Between those bursts of energy and defiant excursions in the saddle she was an increasingly sick woman. On the one hand, the expected child was long in coming, and on the other, the case which her beloved mother had initiated for her, and which she herself had so indomitably carried on, had been decided at last, and decided in favour of her adversaries, and there was nothing more that she could do. Any further attempt by her to enforce her claim in the courts would provoke the enforcement of the penalty-clause, and she would lose everything. She was defeated, and disappointed, and worn out, and she was not quite twenty-eight.

The child, when it came, was christened Thomas, doubtless after its great-grandfather, that Lord Buckhurst who in his youth had been part-author of the first English blank-verse tragedy, had later been the companion and stand-by of Queen Elizabeth in her last stricken years, and had lived on to become the first Earl of Dorset and to die spectacularly, in a fit of anger, at a meeting of the Privy Council. The mother's state of health, both physical and mental, cannot have been

propitious to the birth of a healthy child, and the little
Lord Buckhurst died in the following July, at five months
old. Things being as they were, it was no time for detailed
diary-keeping. The diarist was ill, the pursuit of her
inheritance was at a standstill, the weather was notably
wet, and the London season uncommonly dull. Chamberlain, writing to Sir Dudley Carleton in April, says, 'We
were never at so low ebb for matter of news, specially
public', a race between two footmen, from St. Albans to
Clerkenwell, being as fully attended as if it were a great
Court occasion, simply because there was nothing else
to do in the way of diversion. The weather was bad,
the going was worse, the King's footman won 'by main
strength', his opponent collapsing near Highgate, some
of the noble spectators fell off their horses into the
mud, because of the crowds and the confusion, and
most people came home looking a good deal the worse
for wear. There was a fantastic amount of betting, but
it was no use pretending that it had been a brilliant
or successful occasion.

The other major event of the year had been the return
of Sir Walter Ralegh from his abortive expedition to
Guiana. He had not found the gold-mine he went to
look for, he had lost his son in a conflict with the
Spaniards, he was utterly broken in health, and his
hopes for the future were proved to have died, as he
suspected, with young Prince Henry. He had been famous,
and he was a failure, and for many people in office he
would be better out of the way, so his 15-year-old
conviction was invoked against him, and he went back
to the Tower. Even there, he could not return to the
quarters where he had made himself a home; they were
now occupied by the imprisoned Somersets, and he had
to be accommodated elsewhere. But this inconvenience
was not to last for long; the sorry business was best
brought to an end as soon and as unobtrusively as could
be contrived, and on Lord Mayor's Day, when it was
hoped that London in general would be crowding to
the pageantry of the City and have no eyes for other

events, he was led out at Westminster to die. Tower Hill
would have been too near to the crowds and the popular
excitement that the authorities wanted to avoid, so it
was arranged that on the day before the City function he
should make his last appearance before the judges in
Westminster Hall and not go back to the Tower, but
spend the rest of the day, and of his life, in the Gate-house
prison round the corner, and die by the axe next morning
in Old Palace Yard. Dorset's kinsman, Lord Arundel, was
on the scaffold with him, so was the former Lord Hay,
newly raised to the Viscounty of Doncaster, and he met
his end like the great Elizabethan that he was. Chamberlain
wrote a full account of the execution only a few days
afterwards, and Fuller, author of the *Worthies of England,*
was the nephew of that Dean of Westminster who
attended him in his last hours, so that their narratives
of his life and death, from the famous episode of the
cloak spread before the Queen to his giving the word of
command to his hesitant executioner on the scaffold,
have better authority than some of the folk-lore that has
accumulated around the great figures of history.

Altogether, the year 1618 had been a dull and depressing one for many people, and for Lady Anne it had
begun with a late and probably difficult childbirth,
continued in bereavement and closed once again in
the stuffy darkness of a sick-room. The opening words
of the diary, when it begins again, give us a little indication of what must have gone before. 'The 1st of this
month I began to have the curtain drawn in my chamber
and to see light.' A cloth-of-silver cushion embroidered
with the royal arms of Denmark was sent to the Queen
as a New Year gift, and the four-year-old Lady Margaret
was given her first velvet coat, being advanced from her
former red baize to a garment of crimson velvet laced
with silver. The next four days are taken together:
'The 2-3-4-5th I sat up and had many ladies come to
see me, and much other company, and so I passed
the time'. The entry combines with those that follow,
to suggest the formal visits that customarily accompanied

a lying-in, and it seems that in the course of the year
Lady Anne had had time to bear, and lose, another child.
We know that in the course of her marriage to Dorset
she bore him two sons who died in extreme infancy, but
the record gives no dates, only mentioning that the five-
month-old Thomas was the only one to live any length
of time. No names are assigned to the others, which
indicates that they did not live long enough to be
christened.

She passed the time of her convalescence in going
through a great trunk of miscellaneous letters and papers
of her mother's—letters from friends, documents about
the property in Westmorland and Craven, and miscellaneous philosophical treatises—and seeing visitors who
talked to her on all subjects. Her old friend Lady
Wotton spent most of an afternoon with her in 'much
conference of old matters and of the *Matthew* business',
next day came a whole string of noble visitors, including
a 'young Lady *Donne*' who discussed religion, and on
the day after that there was a family dinner-party, with
her three sisters-in-law, Lord Russell and Sir Edward
Gage, followed by calls from still more friends, who
told her 'a great deal of news'. Dorset himself had just
lost a lot of money at play with the King, and had gone
down to Knole a week or ten days before, so his lady
was on her own at Great Dorset House, obviously very
weak still, but able to take an interest in things around
her and enjoy the company of her friends. On the eve
of her departure from London she even arranged a small
family supper-party for her sisters-in-law, Lady Compton,
and her estranged husband, with her other kinfolk,
Lady Beauchamp, Bess Neville and Tom Glenham, in
the hope of bringing the Comptons together again. A
marginal note implies that they were in fact reconciled
at about this time, whether or not she had anything to
do with it.

When she went down to Knole she was still too weak
to sit upright in a jolting coach, and travelled accordingly
in a litter, an easier method of conveyance for those in

poor health. Slung between two horses, before and behind, it enabled the occupant to recline, or even lie at full length, and there was no jarring of wheels to shake the whole framework, since it was suspended from the harness of the sure-footed horses and made no contact itself with the stony and uneven ground. It could not be easily taken on board a raft or barge, and accordingly Lady Anne went through the City and over London Bridge, while the child, who was travelling in a coach, was ferried across the Thames. Even so, the journey must have been something of an ordeal, and it is not surprising to read that on arrival 'All this week I kept my chamber, because I found myself ill and weak'. After that came the end of the month, and her birthday. She was still only twenty-nine.

The diary entries are only intermittent now. The 8th of February was Shrove Tuesday, and she notes that 'that day I made pancakes with my women in the Great Chamber', and two days later Walter Coniston began to read St. Augustine's *De Civitate Dei* aloud to her, as suitable reading-matter for Lent. The day was marked, at the same time, by the arrival of a letter from Davis the agent, enclosing one from Ralph Coniston about affairs in the north. Lord William Howard was at odds with the Cliffords over some question or other, and had summoned them before the Council to answer for it. Lady Anne was not ill-natured, but she could not help noting this with satisfaction. So long as those differences continued, there would be no risk of the two great north-country factions of Clifford and Howard uniting against her. If once they settled down on good terms as neighbours, and accepted the present arrangements as comfortable and satisfactory for all parties, nobody would be anxious for, or even interested in, the return of the property to its rightful owner. Obstinacy is hard to move, but general complacency is harder still, and this continued unrest, however slight was correctly estimated, in a marginal note by the diarist, as 'a very good matter for me'.

She began Lent by fasting very strictly, abstaining even from butter and eggs, but she was not yet well enough for such activity, and after 10 days her husband persuaded her to stop it. Her own admission is that she 'looked very pale and ill, and was very weak and sickly' which in the circumstances is not surprising. News from Westmorland continued to be favourable, according to reports from Davis and from Marsh, and her family and connections in London were chiefly concerned with Lady Suffolk's illness and with the Lake case, which was coming to a head as a major fashionable scandal.

Sir Thomas Lake, from the very beginning of the reign, had been as notorious and indefatigable a place-hunter as Bacon himself. For some time he had attached himself to the Howards and had their support in his efforts to succeed Robert Cecil, Earl of Salisbury, as Secretary of State, but he was always ready to turn his coat for his own advancement, and was supposed to have been instrumental in introducing George Villiers to the King, in the hope of rising to office under the protection of the new favourite. On Salisbury's death there was much furious canvassing for the Secretaryship, which eventually went to Sir Ralph Winwood, but Lake was sworn a Privy Councillor, and later became joint Secretary with Winwood and his successor Naunton. His wife was equally well known for passionate ambition and intrigue, and they had established a connection with Salisbury's family by marrying their daughter to William Cecil, Lord Roos, grandson of the Earl of Exeter. Lady Anne had made a note of the wedding at the time, as the Howard connection gave it a certain family interest, but since then, Roos had been sent abroad on an embassy and had died in Italy, and rumour said that his widow was now to marry her late husband's cousin, Lord John Paulet, son and heir to the Marquess of Winchester. There had been trouble in the family in his lifetime; Chamberlain in 1617 had reported that Roos had complained to his father-in-law, Sir Thomas, about 'the diabolical dealings of the Lady Lake', but since then she had gone beyond all bounds. She and her husband had started a rumour that the Countess of Exeter was trying to poison their daughter; a servant of Lady Exeter's had been decoyed to the Lakes' house for questioning by Sir Thomas and held there ever since, and Lord Exeter in anger had referred the whole matter to the personal judgement of the King.

Chamberlain wrote to Carleton saying frankly that he did not know what to make of it, but that it was naturally incumbent on the lady 'to clear herself from so foul scandals of precontracts, adultery, incest, murder, poison and suchlike peccadilloes'. In the same letter he apologises for dwelling so long on the subject, but says 'I do only tell you what is said in Paul's'. That fashionable promenading-place, the cathedral nave, was a kind of unofficial club, where the Jacobean man-about-town would take a turn daily, see his friends and acquaintances and exchange small-talk, *bons mots,* political intelligence, accurate or otherwise, or, as in the present instance, plain scandal. The whole affair had been growing to a head in 1618, the year of Lady Anne's illness and withdrawal, and now that she was getting better, her friends were very ready to come and tell her about it, as the King's judgement was given in February in favour of Lady Exeter. The Lakes and Lady Roos were sent to the Tower and sentenced to pay heavy fines to the King, and heavy damages to the plaintiff, Sir Thomas was dismissed from the Secretaryship, and a maid, Sarah Swarton, who claimed to have heard Lady Exeter admit her guilt, was sentenced to be fined, pilloried, whipped and branded as a false accuser, but this sentence was not carried out because she confessed at the last moment that the charges were forged, though even at that point she refused to name the actual forger, having sworn on the Sacrament to keep silence. She was able, on the other hand, to supply information about the habits and character of Lady Roos, which Lady Anne described as 'exceedingly foul matters' affecting the happiness of one Lettice Lake, who had married the Lakes' son Arthur and was about to bear a child.

Dorset's own health was none too good at this time. He had gone up to London on horseback, as heavy snow made the roads impossible for coaches, and 'was so ill after his journey that whereas he intended to return (in) two or three days he stay'd nine or ten'. His brother Edward had a dangerous fever likewise, and the Queen, who had been ailing for some time, died on 2 March. A few weeks later the King was so ill at Newmarket that for some time his recovery was doubtful, and Prince Charles went hurriedly down to see him. Most of the great ladies of the Court went into mourning, and even though King James did not die, it came in useful for appearing as watchers at the Queen's lying-in-state at Denmark House. In due course Lady Anne was to take her turn both at watching by the body and at walking as a mourner in the funeral procession, the two things she had not been allowed to do at Queen Elizabeth's funeral 15 years before, but in the meantime it seems that her Lenten fasting had been rather too much for her, and she was physically and emotionally exhausted. On the evening of Good Friday she 'fell in a great passion of weeping', and declared she was not fit to take communion at Easter as she had meant to do. She said so next day to the chaplain, and her husband accordingly arranged that there should be no family communion in the chapel at Knole, but that those of the household who wished to do so should make their Easter communion at the parish church. By that same afternoon Lady Anne was feeling very much better and was quite sorry to have caused the postponement, particularly as her husband was making himself very pleasant to her and arranging to safeguard her interests if she would come to an arrangement about the alloca- tion of her personal allowance. The slight alarm had blown over, he went down to Lewes to see the spring parade or 'muster', and his lady noted with satisfaction that the Sussex authorities had prepared it 'in so much better fashion by reason of their affection to him, which was as much as my Lord hath in any county or can have'. Quarrels apart, she still took a great pride and pleasure in his achievements and the way in which they were recognised and appreciated by all who knew him.

With the approach of summer it seemed that things were looking up. The King was still a very sick man, but had been pronounced to be out of danger, and a service of thanksgiving for his recovery had been held at Paul's Cross. Dorset was advised to pay him a visit at Royston, since nearly everybody else had done so, and his absence, though due to his own ill-health, would have been noticed. He complied, with satisfactory results, as 'the King used him very well', and he stayed there for a few days before returning to London. Lady Anne came up on the following Saturday to join him and began a round of social engagements, calling on various friends and showing them her new suit of Court mourning, taking a turn at sitting by the dead Queen's body at Somerset House and attending the christening of a friend's child, where her husband was one of the godfathers. News from the north was still encouraging; Lord Clifford was not endearing himself to the tenants, and two of them came up to London and called on Lady Anne to support them in some litigation against his father, Lord Cumberland. There were more new clothes, still in the fashionable Court mourning, and a joint visit to friends and relatives in the Tower, first going to see Lady Somerset and her little daughter, and then dividing, Dorset to wait upon the Earl of Northumberland, and his lady, with Lady Windsor, to Lady Shrewsbury, who was still technically a prisoner, though allowed by this time a considerable degree of latitude. After supper that same evening the Dorsets took a boat and went upstream to Cannon Row stairs by Whitehall, to call on Lord Hertford and his lady (who was another Howard cousin), and Lady Anne finished the evening at Arundel House talking to Lady Shrewsbury's daughter 'about Lords being made Knights of the Garter' —an honour that Lord Dorset naturally hoped and angled for, but never attained.

Her relation with the Cliffords continued as a kind of uneasy truce. Lord Cumberland she hardly ever saw, but

Lord Clifford was on friendly terms with her husband
and could not be ignored. On the other hand, she was in
strong sympathy with John and Richard Dent of King's
Meaburn, the two tenants against whom Clifford was
taking legal proceedings. At the beginning of May
Mr. Davis the agent came and read to her and Lord Dorset
the text of the formal action that was to be brought in
the Court of Chancery, and a week later the parties duly
appeared in court before Lord Chancellor Bacon, who
came down heavily on the side of the Cliffords and made
little of the Dorsets' claim for tenants' rights. They were
'much perplexed and troubled', but Lady Anne characteristically refused to be daunted by this rebuff, apparently with the encouragement of the aged Master of the
Rolls, Sir John Taylor, who had been her father's friend.
Lord William Howard came round a few days later and
had an hour's talk with her, promising to help in any
way he could. As Lady Anne had been told, he was at
present on no good terms with his northern neighbours,
which did something to counteract the fact that Dorset
and Lord Clifford were getting on very well together,
being constant companions at sporting and social events,
summed up in the diary as 'running at the ring and going
to Hyde Park and those places'.

On 13 May the Queen's funeral took place at last. It
was very large, very expensive and, according to the
ever-useful John Chamberlain, very dull to watch. There
were numbers of noble mourners and still larger numbers
of professionals and 'an army of mean fellows that were
servants to the Lords and others of the train', but they
were all dressed alike, and 'came laggering along, even tired
with the length of the way and weight of their clothes'
so that the general effect was tedious and exhausting
rather than impressive. Lady Anne walked hand in hand
with Lady Lincoln, each of them in a mourning dress
containing 16 yards of black broadcloth—the official
allowance for countesses. Lord Dorset and Lord Clifford
were also there, the latter carrying one of the banners,
and there seems to have been some opportunity for

social conversation. The diary, at any rate, notes that
'at the funeral I met with my old Lady Pembroke and
divers others of my acquaintances with whom I had
much talk', and there is no word of complaint or exhaus-
tion. Whoever it was whom Chamberlain had seen lagging
and staggering, we may be reasonably sure it was not
Lady Anne.

Indeed, the day was not over yet. While she was up at
Westminster, she took the opportunity of paying another
visit to old Lord Hertford and pleading with him—unsuc-
cessfully—on behalf of one Wood, to whom it would seem
that some member of the family owed money, as the old
gentleman's reply was a flat refusal to arrange for the
settlement of any of his grandchildren's debts after his
death. Then on her return home there was a visit to Lady
Beauchamp to display her suit of full ceremonial mourning, and the evening ended at last with a great supper
given by Lord Dorset to some members of the French
Ambassador's suite. The meal was followed by a play,
and the play by a banquet—not, as in the modern sense,
a heavy and elaborate meal, but what we should call a
buffet-supper—for the people who had been asked to the
play but not to the dinner-party that had gone before it.
For two months and more, while the Queen's body lay
above ground, her players had been prohibited from
performing in public, and they had suffered an additional
loss by the death of Richard Burbage, their leading actor,
so they would have every reason to be grateful for a
private engagement in the house of a great nobleman.
For one thing, they would be well paid for the performance itself, and for another, it was a good chance of
showing their quality, at the earliest possible moment,
now that the ban on performances was over and they
would soon be appearing again before the London public.

Only one member of this select audience is singled
out for mention by Lady Anne, a Lady Penniston, whose
name has not appeared earlier in the diary. From later
reference it is clear that this lady was Lord Dorset's
current mistress, and their attachment may well account

for his frequent absences from Knole or odd visits to London. Lady Anne may well have known of it, just as she had known of her father's intrigue with 'a lady of quality' many years before, but she had not been required, up to now, to receive such a person at Dorset House and treat her with the courtesy due to a guest. Even at Knole, in the succeeding months, she could not keep clear of the association, for in a footnote to the diary at the end of July she notes that the lady had spent all the summer 'drinking the waters' at Tunbridge Wells, a fact that had caused a lot of talk in the neighbourhood, and some severe criticism of Lord Dorset.

Meanwhile, in London, she was assiduous to do all she could for those whom she still regarded as her tenants and dependants in the north. Two days after the funeral she went by water to call on Lord Carew at the *Savoy* and 'spoke to him very earnestly in behalf of *Peter Coolinge* and his son for a gunner's place in *Carlisle* and received a reasonable good answer from him'. They had planned to go down into Kent after the festivities, but the journey was put off because of a sudden storm of rain —serious not only in itself but for its effect on unmetalled country roads where a heavy coach would get into difficulties—and Dorset took his lady instead to Westminster Abbey to see the place where the Queen had been finally buried after the elaborate ceremony was over.

Lady Anne stayed to see the royal tombs, as she had done three years before, on the eve of that exhausting family session over her inheritance. Now she was not 10 days short of the third anniversary of her mother's death, and must have occupied her mind with thoughts of the monument she had commissioned to be set up over her grave. Appleby church was far away; by 1617, when the tomb was completed, she herself was no longer Lady of Brougham, she had never seen it, and still had 30 years to wait before she did. Her diary of the time contains no allusion to the splendid monument at Appleby, but from the first she had been obviously determined that something should be done, and done in the best manner possible, and its whole appearance is reminiscent of the royal and noble tombs at Westminster. The dead Countess lies at full length in Nottingham alabaster, her hands joined in prayer and her feet just clear of a recumbent lamb. Her close-bodied doublet, buttoned down the front, is clearly worn over the hip-roll known as a French farthingale, but the lower part is hidden by the sweeping folds of a widow's mantle, elaborately pleated, that covers her from head to foot and is brought round and crossed over her form, just below waist level, like the royal mantle in Maximilian Colte's effigy of Queen Elizabeth. Indeed, there is much about the appearance of the whole monument that supports the belief that it is in fact Colte's work, and that Lady Anne paid tribute to her mother's memory by studying the tombs of the greatest in the land and commissioning the work from the artist whom she and many others considered the best that could be had.

In its early years, and indeed up to the 19th century, the tomb was surrounded by a railing, and to this feature may be due the fact that, unlike many others of its kind, the effigy still retains its coronet of gilded metal. The tomb-chest itself is of black and white marble, with carved and painted escutcheons of arms at both ends, and memorial inscriptions in panels on the long sides, between pilasters carved with emblems of mortality in high relief. The face is a finely-modelled piece of portraiture, almost certainly copied from a death-mask, as examination from directly above (from which no ordinary spectator would have been able to look at it) shows that it is without ears, an omission concealed from the casual observer by the side-curls of hair and the folds of the mantle that screen it on each side.

It was only in 1884 that the momument was moved to its present position in the north-east chapel of the parish church. Before that, it stood in the Sanctuary, just south of the centre line, and presumably balanced the communion table, which in the 17th century would have been placed end-on, running east and west. When

in later years this was re-sited across the eastern end of
the church, the position of the tomb rendered it both
unsightly and inconvenient for the administration of
the Sacraments, and as it showed signs of subsidence and
cracking, a faculty was obtained for its removal, its former
position being marked by an inscribed stone in the pavement of the Sanctuary. Comment was aroused, when it
was taken up, by the discovery that there was no sign of
body, bones or lead coffin beneath it, the ground on
which the base-slab had rested being merely dry mould.
On the north side, however, was the edge of a stone
slab, apparently of some antiquity, suggesting the existence of a grave beneath, and it would seem indeed that
the presence of such a hollow under one side only had
caused the cracking by preventing the even subsidence
of the whole monument, most of which rested upon
undisturbed and solid earth. There was no occasion, and
no justification, for disturbing the ground to the north
of the tomb and uncovering the entire stone and what
lay beneath, but it suggests very strongly that the actual
grave was in the very centre of the east end, immediately
before the present altar, and that from the outset the
monument had not been placed directly on top of it,
but to one side, overlapping it only by a very narrow
margin. It is clear from Lady Anne's own account of
the arrangements that there was no question of the body
being laid in a vault previously prepared for it; the actual
place of burial was not decided by the Countess herself
but left to her daughter's discretion, and the elaborate
tomb and effigy rested, not on a firm base of subterranean
masonry, but on the edge and environs of an ordinary
grave.

Two days later the weather had cleared up, the roads
were drier and the whole household went down to Knole.
Before she left, Lady Anne saw her two Westmorland
tenants for the last time and gave them presents and
encouragement, but her support was of no help to them
in their action. When she was out of the way, they were
summoned before the Lord Chancellor. Bacon told them

roundly that they were to be good tenants to Lord Cumberland, and sharply reprimanded Davis, Lady Anne's agent, for his part in the affair.

The diary becomes rather spasmodic at this point. Several days are taken together and record only that 'I went abroad with my brother *Sackville,* sometimes early in the morning and sometimes after supper, he and I being kind and having better correspondence than we have had'. This itself is a surprising admission, since she usually distrusted her brother-in-law and never had a good word for him. On the last day of May she 'stayed at home and was sad and melancholy', and apparently took the opportunity to write up her diary by adding a long footnote about miscellaneous events that had not been entered at the time of their occurrence. Lady Roos had made formal acknowledgement of her guilt and received a pardon, but her parents remained obdurate and were 'committed close prisoners to the Tower for contempt of Court'. Lord William Howard had begun a Star Chamber action against some supporters of the Cliffords, and there was a rumour that a suit was to be brought against Thomas Howard, Earl of Suffolk (her husband's uncle, and father of Lady Somerset) and even that Lord Dorset might be included in it, but that proceedings were put off for the present. Dorset himself had some lavish entertainment, had been very successful with his fighting-cocks and had won a great deal of money. On the 27th she had walked with him after supper

> before the gate where I told him how good he was to everybody else and how unkind to me. In conclusion he promised me in a manner that he would make me a jointure of four thousand pounds a year, whereof part should be of the land he has assured to my uncle *Cumberland.*

Altogether it is a disjointed and rather pathetic little summary, set down almost at random on a 'sad and melancholy' day.

The failure of that attempt to support her mother's tenants must have meant much to Lady Anne. Her diary-keeping is no longer systematic, the entries are few, listless and irrelevant, and it seems that even her indomitable spirit had come near to breaking under the strain and the frustration. On one or two days in June she had the energy to rise at four o'clock in the morning and go riding, and on the 24th of the month she notes that 'my Lord received the last payment of my portion which was £6,000, so as he hath received in all £17,000'. And that, from her point of view, was all he was going to get. The final payment of £3,000 was due at Michaelmas, but it was to be contingent on her making formal acceptance of the award as a just settlement of all claims, and in view of her known and inflexible resolution never to surrender her rights in Westmorland there seems to be neither evidence nor justification for Dr. Williamson's easy assumption that 'the payment probably was made'. As a married woman she could not control her own money, but by refusing to surrender her principles she could prevent herself, and consequently her husband, from getting any more of it, and that, it appears, is what she did. It is significant that on 21 September she notes that she spent all the week with her sisters-in-law, 'being sad about an unkind letter from my Lord'. Michaelmas was on the 29th, and it looks very much as if he had made one last attempt at persuasion and strongly resented her refusal to comply.

It had not been an easy summer after all. The Clifford cousins must have been encouraged, and Lady Anne's hopes correspondingly depressed, by the fact that Lady Clifford was expecting a child. If it should be a boy, he would become heir to the Westmorland estates, and Lady Anne's chance of succession would be deferred for another generation, possibly beyond her own lifetime, if the longevity of the current Lord Cumberland was anything to go by. Still, she, too, had an heir, though not a son. Lady Margaret was five years old at the beginning of July, her birthday was marked by general health-drinking and her father commissioned Paul Van Somer to paint her portrait, and subsequently his own. Towards the end of the month Lady Clifford's son was born, and was hastily christened Francis, but lived only a few hours. The fact is noted in the diary, but without the note of personal advantage which accompanies the news of the Cliffords' difficulties with their tenants or differences with Lord William Howard. Lady Anne had known what it was to bear, and lose, a little son, and indeed she was soon to know it again. In August she was fretful and quarrelsome, and matters were not improved by her having to entertain, among others, Sir Thomas and Lady Penniston, who came to stay for a couple of nights, 'there being great entertainment and much stir about them'. September brought the crisis of Michaelmas and the consequent 'unkind letter from my Lord', and with October came the realisation that another child was on the way.

This time we hear no more of clothes and Court visits. The Queen was dead, the Prince not yet married, and there was little or nothing to tempt or summon fashionable society to Whitehall. Lady Anne was once again a sick woman. She stood at her window one evening when 'the Fire Dog play'd with fire'—a phrase which Dr. Williamson interprets as referring to a fire-extinguisher of some sort, but seems more likely to denote a trained animal giving a performance in the courtyard—and caught a cold, for summer was gone, and it was October now. At the end of the month she was not well enough to leave her room, and notes that she stayed in it till the 23rd of the following March, but found the time passed by more quickly than it had done when she was out and about. Matters in Westmorland were not going well, her husband's uncle, the Earl of Suffolk, had been found guilty of misappropriating public money, had been dismissed from office and sent, with his Countess, to the Tower— though this imprisonment lasted only for ten days—and Lord Dorset was living in London as a gay and hospitable grass-widower 'drawing a great company of Lords and gentlemen that used to dine with him'. On the other hand, the end of the month seems to have seen the last of his intrigue with Lady Penniston. Life still had its consolations, and Lady Anne was still able to appreciate them.

And so the year draws on to its end. The neighbours were kind, Lord Dorset came to Knole, and Lady Anne listened to reading and saw one or two visitors. One Sunday there was no sermon because the chaplain was at Oxford, but Sir Ralph Boswell came to dinner, and played and sang to his hostess in the afternoon. Dorset gave his lady three shirts, presumably to be made up into baby-linen for the expected child, and they both signed a power of attorney for Ralph Coniston to collect the debts that were still due to the dowager Lady Cumberland's estate in the north. This inevitably revived the old antagonism between them, and there was a bitter quarrel that same evening, 'he saying that if ever my land came to me I should assure it as he would have me'. The loss of that final payment of £3,000 was naturally still rankling.

All the same, the quarrel blew over, as others had done. Three nights later, Dorset took supper with his lady in her quarters, and though he seems to have gone up to London for Christmas, he sent for a pedigree of the Sackvilles, for which she wrote him a letter of thanks on Boxing Day. There were the great family chronicles to be studied, furs, that had come down from London, to be unpacked and aired, and the ordinary calm routine of listening to reading and playing back-gammon with the steward, but the suit for the inheritance was at an end, and the Knole diary ends with it.

Chapter Nine

INTERLUDE, AND A PICTURE

I must be patient till the heavens look
With an aspect more favourable
The Winter's Tale, II, i

THERE IS NO DETAILED record of Lady Anne's life
in the years that followed. Her son was born, but did
not live long enough for baptism, a daughter was born
in 1622 and was christened Isabella, and two years later
Lord Dorset died of what would appear to have been
dysentery—brought on, according to Chamberlain, by
'a surfeit of potatoes'. This might seem surprising, but
for the fact that the word was used by Chamberlain—as
by Falstaff in Windsor Park—to denote not the vegetable
of present-day cookery, but the American sweet-potato,
much in demand as a luxury and an aphrodisiac. Dorset
continued in his high living to the last, and on the very
day of his death he dictated and signed an affectionate
letter to his wife, reassuring her that he was getting better,
that she was not to worry, but that he would write to her
every day and let her know when she could come to see
him. She herself was far from well at the time, and was
down at Knole, looking after the nine-year-old Lady
Margaret, who was sickening for what turned out to be
smallpox. Lady Anne caught the disease from her, and
though they both recovered, she felt that her looks were
utterly ruined, and that she could never think of marrying
again.

When she was able to move, she and her children left
Knole for Chenies, the seat of her mother's people, and
Great Dorset House for a series of London houses in
Westminster or St. Bartholomew's. Her brother-in-law
and his wife were Earl and Countess of Dorset now,
and she, at 34, had become Countess Dowager. She and
her husband had been lovers from the day of their

marriage, when they were barely out of their 'teens. They had quarrelled furiously, as lovers may, and hurt each other deeply, as lovers can, with their passion intensifying their injustice and unkindness, but those outbursts are recorded only in the notes made at the time of each. Lady Anne's allusions to her husband, and her memories of him recorded in tranquillity, show her affection and admiration unfaltering to the very end.

In her widowhood, she followed her mother's example in taking steps in good time to provide for the future of her daughters. In 1628 she entered a formal claim to her right of succession to the Clifford estates—not to upset the present holders, in breach of the King's award, but to make quite clear that in the absence of male issue they were entailed upon her and her descendants. There was to be no repetition, if she could help it, of her father's action in leaving the property out of the lawful line. And it was not too soon to take thought for the continuance of that line and arrange a suitable marriage for her elder child. In April 1629, though she was not yet 15, Lady Margaret was married in St. Bartholomew's church to John, Lord Tufton, in due course to become Earl of Thanet, and just over a year later, at the beginning of June 1630, Lady Anne herself married again.

The attack of smallpox had not 'martyred her face' to the extent she feared. She was a well-do-do widow of unimpeachably good family, and with the possibility of succeeding to a great deal of valuable country property. She was only just turned 40, and though small in stature she had great personal dignity and was eminently presentable. And, above all, from the fortune-hunter's point of view, she had no close male relatives to become awkward hangers-on to a successful suitor. There were neither sons nor brothers to claim a share in her fortune. she was on bad terms with her cousin Clifford, and on still worse terms with her brother-in-law, the new Earl of Dorset, so she might be considered a very valuable acquisition for an enterprising nobleman not in his first youth.

From Lady Anne's point of view, likewise, a second husband seemed desirable after all. In her own phrase, she had 'many enemies in the time of her widowhood'. She had had an unpleasant experience in 1626, when burglars tried to break into her house at Chenies just after the collection of her Lady-Day rents. The alarm was given, however, by someone who saw them getting in, and Lady Anne's own account of the attempt implies a strong suspicion that her brother-in-law was at the back of it. In their unprotected state, she and her daughters were too valuable, and too vulnerable, for safety, and she wisely abandoned her first hasty resolution never to re-marry. At first, as she told her secretary in after years, she retained the stipulation that her next husband should not be a courtier, nor already a father (she had been bringing up those two illegitimate daughters of her late husband as it was) nor 'a great curser and swearer', but she abandoned this, too, when it came to the point, for the man she married was all three.

On and off, she had known him 20 years and more. When she was a girl, young Philip Herbert, brother of the Earl of Pembroke, had been one of the darling favourites of King James, who had created him Earl of Montgomery. When he had been supplanted by Carr in the Royal affection (through the machinations of Lady Suffolk, who had constituted herself the King's unofficial provider of beautiful young men, besides getting Carr married to her own daughter), he took his supersession calmly and remained on good terms with everyone except the Howards, who had arranged it. His first wife had been one of Lady Anne's fellow-dancers in *Tethys' Festival* in 1610, and he himself had ridden gallantly in the tilt-yard and the hunting-field. He had followed the spirit of the age by encouraging literature without showing the least ability or desire to practise it, he could barely read or write, but was a sound judge of pictures, sculpture, architecture, and, in his younger days, human nature, and Aubrey records that 'his chiefe delight was in Hunting and Hawking, both which he had to the greatest perfection of any Peer in the Realm'. He had been sent on the King's behalf to visit Lady Somerset, his rival's wife, in the Tower, and had himself received her admission of guilt in instigating Overbury's murder, and he had been one of the few intimates in attendance on that momentous occasion when King James took it upon himself to decide the matter of the Clifford inheritance, and Lady Anne withstood him to his face. Now he was a middle-aged widower, between 40 and 50, still in high favour with the King, and by his brother's death he had lately become Earl of Pembroke. On many counts he might be reckoned a very suitable husband for an unprotected widow, an heiress and the mother of heiresses, as he was well born, well known to her, well placed at Court and, though he made no claim to elegance in those days, women still found him attractive.

And that, perhaps, was where the trouble began. Lady Anne knew, or thought she knew, the habits of married men; both her father and her first husband had had their independent love affairs, but she was not prepared for anything on the scale of Pembroke's infidelities. They cannot have been open and flagrant, or he would not have retained, as he did, the favour and near-friendship of the eminently proper King Charles. Even Court gossip about him related to his quarrelsome and violent nature rather than to his miscellaneous amours, but John Aubrey's papers contain one or two odd notes about the family, and it seems possible that the two brothers, both of them 'immoderately given to women', may have been affected by the somewhat peculiar interest he attributes to their mother. Be that as it may, Lady Anne remained his wife for 20 years, but lived with him for less than five. While he retained his quarters at the Cockpit in Whitehall, she lived apart from him at Wilton or when she had to be in London, at Baynard's Castle in the City. Even so, she made careful enquiries, both directly and indirectly, before coming up to London, in case her husband did not approve. A letter of hers to the Earl of Bedford in 1638 shows that there had been

one occasion when she came up to Whitehall without
his leave, and he roundly turned her out of the house.
It is a justifiable assumption that his London arrangements were not such as to welcome the presence of his
wife. It was better that she should stay down in the
country, with his grown-up children and his brother's
widow, the Dowager Countess of Pembroke, who is
reported by Aubrey to have been out of her mind.

There was no open breach. Lady Anne's summary of
her own life says merely that 'by reason of some discontent' she left Whitehall for Baynard's Castle on
18 December 1634. Possibly his Christmas arrangements
were not to her taste, which would account for the rather
unexpected choice of date, if she was not prepared to
appear as hostess to the kind of house-party he might
be planning to entertain. They still made official
appearances together now and then; in 1632 and 1637
they jointly signed formal claims to the Clifford estates,
and would probably have renewed their claim in 1642
had it not been for the outbreak of the Civil War.

Van Dyck's great family group, still hanging in the
Double Cube room at Wilton, shows Lady Anne seated
full-face, with her arms lightly folded, looking straight
out at the spectator and apparently oblivious of the
splendid figures of her husband and step-children who
stand around her in attitudes calculated to display them
at their best. Lord Pembroke's second wife is dressed
almost humbly in comparison; there is nothing self-
assertive about her attitude or appearance, but her very
detachment gives her something of the quality of
Leonardo's *Gioconda*, and does much to explain the
impression she made on so fastidious a person as George
Herbert, her husband's kinsman and, for a time, his
chaplain. She had been through much, and endured much,
by the time that portrait was painted, and its air of
patience and grave independence goes well with the
simile used by her cousin, Francis Russell, Earl of Bedford.
when he compared her character to the current of the
Rhone, flowing through the lake of Geneva but never

mingling with it or losing its own identity. This cousin was obviously a perceptive man and a good friend in need, since it was he who persuaded Lord Pembroke, after the separation, to settle on Lady Anne the jointure-lands he had originally assigned to his first wife, and to renounce, in favour of her younger daughter, his rights in the Westmorland property, and £5,000 of the Skipton property, if ever she should come into it. Van Dyck's keen eye and cunning hand have caught and preserved for us Pembroke's own high-strung and passionate nature; were he a horse or a hound, that look in the eye, and nervous tension of the muscles about the mouth, would write him down as dangerous, and it is a great tribute to Bedford's mediation that he should have been persuaded to set his hand to such an agreement.

At one time it may have seemed that Lady Anne's second marriage was going to be a mere repetition of the first, with its long periods of lonely wretchedness occupied by reading, prayer and needlework, but very soon a new experience, and a new interest, entered into her life. The King and Queen had always been fond of Wilton, and had regularly stayed there in the time of the late Lord Pembroke, though he himself had never particularly cared for it. Now that it had passed into his brother's possession, there was a chance for those who appreciated it to make the most of its possibilities. It was King Charles who suggested alterations, and the new Earl who enthusiastically accepted the suggestions and put them into practice. Inigo Jones was still the first architect of his day, and was naturally the man to be approached, but he had a great deal of work on his hands, for the King at Whitehall and Greenwich, and for Lady Anne's uncle Lord Bedford on his elaborate piece of residential town-planning at Covent Garden. Though Jones's name is popularly associated with Wilton, and his well-known style is visible in it, he can have done little more than exercise a general supervision, and the real architects of the work seem to have been his pupil, John Webb, and his one-time partner, Isaac de Caus. It was

characteristic of de Caus, certainly, to have spent much
of his time, care and talent on the lay-out of the immense
formal gardens that were to form the foreground for the
new, gigantic south front of the house. Lady Anne found
herself living at Ramsbury more often than at Wilton,
because Wilton was full of architects, designers, con-
tractors and miscellaneous workmen, all busily engaged
on the work of pulling it to pieces and rebuilding it into a
dwelling of even greater beauty than before. It was uninhabitable, for a time, but at the same time it must have
been fascinating. The architect and his associates formed
a link, however, tenuous, with those days more than
20 years earlier, when Inigo Jones had designed her dresses
for the masques in which she had danced and postured
under Ben Jonson's direction, before she was a bride.

All this was a new experience to her, and one that
left an ineradicable impression. Never before had she had
a chance to see at such close range, and on such a scale,
the work of design, demolition, and rebuilding. She
had long been interested in such things, but her study up
to now had been limited mainly to monumental sculpture,
as exemplified by the tombs built at her expense for her
cousin, Frances Bourchier, in 1612, and her mother in
1617, and the memorial to Edmund Spenser that she set
up in 1620 in Westminster Abbey. Now she had a chance
to see what could be done in the way of altering a whole
house, and how one should set about it. To this period,
and this enlarging of her interest and her technical experience, Westmorland may be indebted for her unflagging
work in later years among the great castles of the north,
and the ancillary buildings that surrounded them.

It was in such matters, too, that she found most in
common with her husband. Uncouth and illiterate as
he might be, he had an innate love and understanding of
pictures, architecture and statuary. He and King Charles
were renowned as active and discriminating collectors,
his new wife had often found pleasure in studying the
tomb-sculpture in Westminster Abbey or the collection
of classical statuary formed by her first husband's cousin

at Arundel House. This was something very far removed from his unsavoury pursuits at Whitehall, or those fits of screaming fury that led to his making an exhibition of himself and laying about him with his staff of office as Lord Chamberlain, to the extent of driving Lord Maltravers, at a House of Lords Committee, to retaliate with an inkstand. His picture-buying, and his patronage of architects and portrait-painters, formed a direct link with those artistic activities with which he had been associated when first she knew him, and which had allowed her, in those early, impressionable years, continually to see him at his best.

Something else, too, happened in 1631 and gave her great and lasting pleasure. Her daughter Margaret, the beloved 'child' of the Knole diary gave birth to a son. She herself was still only 16, but in due course she was to bear nine other children, all of whom lived to grow up. For her mother, the arrival of this first grandchild meant a lessening of anxiety and a widening of interest for the future. The line was continuing; there was an heir, and a male heir at that, in the third generation, and she herself, so assiduous in tracing the history of her Clifford ancestors through all the years, might now look forward to watching, guiding and recording the history of her descendants. She herself bore two sons to her new husband, but they did not live, and it was left to her daughters to carry on her line, even as she had carried on her father's.

The Clifford estates came one step nearer in January 1641, with the death of her uncle Francis, in his 82nd year. He had been a careful, kindly man, and the property had done well under his administration, but of late years he had been largely under the thumb of his son, the 'cousin Clifford' who succeeded him as fifth Earl of Cumberland. If he should prove as long-lived as his father, Lady Anne would have little chance of coming into her own, and that little was lessened, a few months later, by the death of another kinsman, Francis Russell, Earl of Bedford, on whose advice and protection she had come increasingly to rely.

Matters were further complicated, at this time, by the increasing tension between King and parliament, soon to come to a head with the outbreak of the Civil War. Despite his long intimacy with King James and his successor, Pembroke took the side of the parliament. Lady Anne remained, as always, an uncompromising Royalist, and this fact, while at times it might be considered an embarrassment, enabled Pembroke to keep a foot in either camp. Their differences had never attained the scale of open scandal, and though they had lived apart for years, it was largely a matter of mutual convenience, and there was nothing against their being seen together in public if they chose. In October 1642 they came up together from Wilton, he to Whitehall and she to Baynard's Castle, where she remained for nearly seven years— the longest time, she says, that she ever lived continually under one roof. The house was old, but stoutly built and luxuriously furnished, and in those troubled times it afforded a reasonably safe harbourage for Lady Anne's person and much of her husband's property, so that the arrangement appeared reasonably satisfactory all round.

It had gone on for just over a year when there came another change in Lady Anne's fortunes. In December 1643 her cousin of Cumberland died, and left no male heir. The earldom became extinct, and the Clifford estates were Lady Anne's at last, after 38 years. It must have seemed a barren victory in many respects, as the war was now in progress in the Midlands, and it was no time for a woman to undertake the long and difficult journey to the north. Her husband's political ties would make it quite impossible for him to go with her, even had he wished to do so, and her younger daughter was now in her early 'twenties and consequently ready for marriage. This was becoming increasingly important, especially as Pembroke had wanted young Isabella, and her £5,000, for one of his own sons, and Lady Anne's refusal had exacerbated the relations between them. She had inherited her rightful property at last, but with things as they were, she could not enter upon her inheritance.

One thing, however, she did, in that of time of waiting, to mark the change in her state. In 1589, the year before she herself was born, her parents had commissioned portraits of themselves and their two elder children, the little brothers who died young. She now conceived the idea of incorporating all these, with others, in one great composite picture illustrative of the descent and last days of the house of Clifford, even as had been done by Holbein for the house of Tudor a hundred years before, and Lucas de Heere in the heyday of Elizabeth. This was no occasion for calling on the services of Van Somer, Mytens or Van Dyck, who had all painted her in their time; the group in the Double Cube Room had been painted from living sitters, but for this enterprise a skilful and ingenious copyist was what was wanted, and the work has been ascribed to Jan van Belcamp. The originals from which he had to work were not, for the most part, full-length figures, and he had to supplement their head-and-shoulder evidence with bodies, costume and accessories based on his own imagination and such material as was available at Baynard's Castle. The composition, therefore, is notable for its historical rather than its aesthetic value.

In the centre panel, some eight feet square, Lord and Lady Cumberland stand with their two little boys. On the wall behind them hang small portraits of his two sisters, the Countess of Derby and Lady Wharton, and her two sisters, Countesses respectively of Warwick and of Bath. Lady Cumberland's face is that of the head-and-shoulders portrait in the National Portrait Gallery—full, calm and almond-eyed, with faint traces of a smile. Her hair grows off the forehead in a pronounced 'widow's peak', and over the back of it she wears a black velvet French hood—a headdress that would be considered distinctly old-fashioned in the days of King James, and not really in the first Court fashion in 1589, when the original portrait was painted. A close collar of pearls is round her neck above the cartwheel ruff of lace, and a long double string of them is draped over her shoulders and caught up with a brooch high on her breast, the slack

hanging down in the middle nearly to her waist. Her dress
is a velvet gown fitting closely in the bodice but with
skirt and sleeves open in front to show a richly-decorated
under-dress of cloth of silver, and adorned with jewelled
clasps down each side of the opening. Its whole outline
is firm and smooth, and it fits practically without a
wrinkle, the skirts of gown and under-dress being borne
out presumably, by the type of bell-shaped petticoat
known as a Spanish farthingale.

Lord Cumberland's head and soft grey-green hat corres-
pond with another head-and-shoulders portrait long in
the possession of the family, but the artist has got into
difficulties further down. The position of the Earl's feet
on the squares of the pavement shows that he is standing
well in front of his wife, but their arms are nevertheless
supposed to be linked, and in consequence his right arm
is twisted back so that the hand rests behind the hip-joint
—a position awkward, and indeed practically impossible,
to attain when wearing armour of the type represented.
The armour itself is rather sketchily indicated; the artist
shows little feeling for its practical construction, though
the details of its star-patterned engravings are given more
fully than in the Hilliard miniature at Greenwich. By 1646,
when this picture was painted, full armour such as this
was out of date. The pieces themselves were still in Lady
Anne's possession, and the painter may well have been
able to see them and copy the design, but he would have
had little or no opportunity to see what they would like
in wear.

The painting of the body-garment emphasises the draw-
back. The jewelled surcoat of the Hilliard miniature fits
closely over the breastplate, but has wide bell-like sleeves
that would allow for the wearing of the customary paul-
drons, or shoulder-pieces, beneath, and their outline is
even indicated under the fabric, but in this later picture
the Earl's grey-green velvet tunic, though supposed to be
worn over armour—one can see it at his neck—could
not have been put on by a man already harnessed. Those
short, puffed sleeves, fitting so closely to the shoulder

and the upper arm, call for a certain suppleness and
agility in the putting on, and suppleness and agility in
that direction are qualities that plate armour was neither
required nor constructed to provide. For forward move-
ment of the arms, in the guidance of a horse and the
manipulation of a weapon, it is admirable, but to square
one's shoulders and put one's arms backward into close-
fitting armholes like these is an impossibility. The painter
has seen the armour, and seen pictures of the body-
garment or something like it, and has assumed in error
that both could be worn together. Quite possibly he was
familiar with that popular historical and geographical
work, John Speed's *Theatre of Great Britain,* and its
elaborately engraved title-page representing the supposed
appearance of an ancient Briton, Saxon, Dane and Norman. The last-mentioned figure is wearing a coat of mail,
of which the sleeves, neck and skirt are visible beneath a
tunic with the full skirts, low neck and puffed shoulder-
sleeves of the beginning of the 16th century. From the
point of view of a mid-17th-century painter, it was an
'antique habit' that would do for any period and would
look quite suitable in the present circumstances. Or,
most likely of all, he saw this actual garment preserved
with the armour and never realised that it was something meant to be worn *under* the cuirass, its padded
shoulders serving to relieve the pressure of the paul-
drons, and Lady Anne herself would have been too
young to know, or to remember, just how her father
armed himself for the tilt-yard at the time of her own
birth.

Across the Earl's breast runs the blue riband of the
Garter, its badge with the figure of St. George being visible
at his left hip, close to the sword-hilt, and the Garter
itself is shown worn about his left knee, over the armour.
One or two faint traces of the engraving and gilding are
visible underneath, suggesting that the leg-armour, with
its engraved design, was painted first, and the Garter put
in afterwards on top of it. Full leg-armour had been
practically discontinued by 1646, so that the artist

might not have known at first, that the actual Garter had
to be included.

The two children are pleasant little full-length figures
in the long coats worn by small boys in Elizabethan days,
but about the two wings of the triptych there is rather
more to be said. The one on the left claims, by its
inscription, to represent Lady Anne at the age of 15,the
other shows her as she presumably was at, or just
before, the time when the picture was painted, and the
combination gives a clue to the significance of the whole
composition. It was at the age of 15 that Lady Anne succeeded, in her mother's opinion and her own, to her
inheritance as the last in the direct line of the Cliffords;
it was only now, at the age of over 50, that she had come
to it in fact and undisputed right.

The younger portrait is a reconstruction from such
material as was available. A miniature by David des
Granges may have furnished, at first or second hand, the
model for the face of Lady Anne in her 'teens, but the
dress and collar represent the fashion of some 10 or 12
years later. The drum-like farthingale of late Elizabethan
and early Jacobean days has given place to a slight padding
about the hips, and the close ruff has been succeeded by
an upstanding collar like a fan, bordering the low neck
of the gown and serving to frame and set forth the lines
of head, neck and low-cut bosom. The dress and its
embroidery are carefully, even delicately painted, as if
from an actual example, and its material, colour and
decoration make allowable a further attempt at identifi-
cation. The material has the sheen of satin, and the colour
is not quite white, but an exceedingly pale green. The
style would have been fashionable in 1617, and it was in
that year that Lady Anne went out of mourning for her
mother and got herself some new dresses, one of them
made of 'sea water green satin' and both of them having
open ruffs of the kind illustrated in the picture. The other
dress was a green damask gown embroidered in gold,
and was the one that she regularly wore at Court 'without
a farthingale' as her figure was changing with the advent

of her short-lived little son. A satin dress like the one
in the picture, however, would not be so adaptable.
Much of its effect depends on its close fit and the play
of light upon its unwrinkled, shining surface, and in
consequence it would have had comparatively little wear,
but would soon have been put away and forgotten, or
preserved because it might come in useful later on. It
was too good—and too small—to be cut up for curtains or
cushions, and by the time Lady Margaret was old enough
to wear it, fashions had changed again and there would
be no point in adapting it for her. By 1646 it might still
be in existence, the earliest new-looking dress available
from Lady Anne's younger days, and available for the
painter to illustrate in a portrait showing her when she
was younger still.

Her hair is dressed over an unseen wire, from which
hangs a series of drop-shaped pearls, and behind this can
be seen the padded, pearl-studded front roll of a small
cap or caul, rather like those seen in portraits of Henri III
of France. A long jewelled chain about her neck is caught
up and fastened at the neck-line of the dress, so that it
is draped in two festoons with the slack hanging nearly
waist-deep between them, a style to be seen in more than
one portrait of her mother.

In the other wing of the triptych she appears again,
but as a very different figure. This is not the girl heiress,
not even the young bride of Knole, nor Van Dyck's noble
chatelaine of Wilton, but the Countess as the artist now
saw her, a woman more than middle-aged, disillusioned by
life and convinced by this time that she has nothing to
look forward to. Her dress is still rich, but it is of plain
black satin, set off with pearls and lace. Her hair is still
dark, but it is thinner than it was, and is draped in black,
as though she were already a widow. The shape of her
head, and the outline of her face, are like her mother's,
and her own youthful portraits, but the firmness and
muscular tension are gone, the cheeks are beginning to
sag, with a suggestion of puffiness and flabbiness, and the
mouth makes no attempt even to pretend to smile. It is a

face without happiness and without hope, and at the same time without any obvious self-pity. She looked like that, and she knew it, and with her unfaltering, uncompromising honesty she let herself be painted so, because it was part of the picture, and part of the story the picture tells. The heiress of Westmorland had been something of a beauty, had shone in the Court and danced in the company of a queen; now the inheritance had come to her at last, and she was a neglected wife, a grandmother and—there was no evading it—a frump.

Like Holbein before and Hogarth after him, the painter has surrounded his sitters with expressive and appropriate accessories, principally books, the titles of which are clearly shown. In the central picture, Lady Cumberland holds a volume of the Psalms, and on the shelf behind her are a Bible, an English translation of Seneca and a manuscript volume of recipes for distillations and home-made medicaments. Her husband has his helmet on a table at his elbow, with his gauntlets hanging below it, and his coat of arms, encircled by the Garter, hangs behind him, under a framed tablet giving a brief account, with dates, of his life and that of his lady. Similar tablets or labels identify the portraits of his and her sisters, a longer inscription appears on a stylised shield held by the elder of the two children, and a brief note about the general composition of the picture is attached to the tablecloth, just below the dangling fingers of the gauntlets.

The side panels, with their portraits of Lady Anne herself, are no less informative. The picture of her in youth includes many of the elements that might be supposed to have formed her character: portraits of her tutor and governess at the top, with two shelves of books below them. There is a Bible, of course, and a number of volumes of poetry, divinity, history and moral philosophy. Samuel Daniel, her tutor, is represented by his poems and his prose history of England; the other poets are Sidney, Spenser, Chaucer and Ovid—the *Metamorphoses*—with the witty satires of Dr. Joseph Hall, whom she is likely to have

known personally, as in his early career he was associated
with a good many of her friends and acquaintances. Significant, in particular, is the inclusion of the Manual of
Epictetus, Boethius' *Consolations of Philosophy* and
Augustine *On the City of God,* all of them works calculated to sustain and encourage patience in adversity. The
objects on the table at the side—an hour-glass, skeins and
reels of coloured silks, a piece of embroidery and a music-
book—suggest the occupations that helped her to pass so
many lonely hours, and leaning up against the table is a
theorbo, a form of lute apparently introduced into this
country by Inigo Jones in the early years of the century.
Its characteristic feature is the double neck, the long
diapason strings, which were not fingered but acted
as extra resonators, being carried on by an extension on
the bass side, extending far beyond the sharply-angled
neck and peg-box of the main set of strings. Finally,
on the floor at her feet and a little behind her, lie four
large folios—Ortelius' atlas, Camden's *Britannia,* Cornelius
Agrippa on the Vanity of the Arts and Sciences and—
perhaps as a counterbalance to the heroic story of the
Crusader Godfrey de Bouillon on the bookshelf—a contemporary work of comic fiction, the satirical *History
of Don Quixote.* Lady Anne knew, and shared, the
pleasure that could be derived from studying the past
and its glories, but she was realist enough to appreciate
that that attitude might be overdone.

On the other side, the background-reading of her contemporary portrait tells a different story. The Bible lies
on the table, convenient to her hand, with an English
translation of Pierre Charron's *Book of Wisdom.* On the
shelves are more volumes of poetry—George Herbert,
Ben Jonson, Fulke Greville, George Sandys' verse translation of the Psalms, and the poems and sermons of her
old acquaintance John Donne—with translations of the
historical works of Guicciardini, Philippe de Commines,
Plutarch and Ammianus Marcellinus, and various volumes
of sermons and meditations on the mortality of mankind.
It looks very much as if she had put the activities of life

behind her and settled down, with her dog and her cat, to meditate upon her latter end. Even so, in a play which she might quite possibly have seen at Court, did Shakespeare's Prospero resolve that on returning to take up his neglected dukedom, 'every third thought should be his grave'.

But Lady Anne was not always right. Though she did not know it, she had 30 years of life ahead of her and they were by no means to be inactive. One book appearing in this part of the picture has no obvious relation to the others, nor to the trains of thought that they represent. On the lower shelf, alongside the works of Plutarch, Greville and Guicciardini, stands *The Element of Architecture*, by Sir Henry Wotton, and its inclusion in unexpected company shows that whether she yet knew it or not, the Countess of Pembroke was developing a new interest. The work of Inigo Jones and his colleagues was bearing unexpected fruit.

As in the other wing she had included portraits of her tutor and her governess, so in this one she stands before the richly-framed likenesses of her two husbands. Each has its appropriate label and biographical note. Lord Dorset's includes a character-sketch and a tribute to his memory; Lord Pembroke, who was still living, is given biographical details alone. The past history of the family, and incidentally of the property, is given in a series of small labels running up each side of the central picture, with the armorial bearings of the persons concerned so far as they could be known.

Two blank shields of fantastic form, near the feet of the two children, stand for Richard Fitz-Punt, who came into England with William the Conqueror, and William his son, who first took the name of Clifford from Clifford Castle in Herefordshire, which was granted to them after the Conquest. Above them, on that side, come the names and arms of the Cliffords of Clifford Castle, with particulars of their estates and marriages, and then those of the various nobles who married Clifford heiresses, from Richard Plantagenet, Earl of

Cambridge, beheaded for conspiracy against Henry V, to John Tufton, Earl of Thanet, and James Compton, Earl of Northampton, who married respectively Lady Margaret and Lady Isabella Sackville, Lady Anne's two daughters by her first husband. The last marriage, in fact, took place in 1647, after the picture had been begun, so that it represented the family descent and connections as brought absolutely up to date.

The other side shows the history of the Westmorland inheritance. It begins, by Lord Cumberland's foot, with the escutcheon and name of Robert de Vipont (given in its latinised form Veteripont), to whom the property had been granted by King John. Above this come those of his son and grandson, and with the marriage of the latter's daughter to Roger de Clifford the succession is shown continued in the Clifford line for over 300 years, culminating in Lady Anne's own marriages at the very top of the border. The one side is an epitome of the descent of the Clifford family; the other, of the Clifford estates, and long explanatory scrolls explain the complications of the succession, with Lady Anne's uncompromising contention that the property was 'wrongfully detayned from her many yeares, by her Unkle the Earle of Cumberland and his sonne'. Whatever may be thought of the quality of its execution, the whole conception is both imaginative and expressive and tells the story of the Clifford inheritance from the standpoint of the last Clifford to hold it. With its combination of verbal and pictorial record, it is in itself a valuable historical document, and very appropriately it now occupies a place of honour in Appleby Castle.

Chapter Ten

THE LAST UPROOTING

These high wild hills and rough uneven ways
Draws out our miles, and makes them wearisome

Richard II, II, iii

MEANWHILE, THERE WAS A good deal to be done, at the London end, about the property and other things. The country was admittedly in a state of civil war, but a discreet messenger could go where a rich noblewoman and her entourage could not, and Lady Anne was able to write to her cousin, Sir John Lowther, about the Westmorland estates, and to send instructions to her tenants there about their rents. First and most important, they were not to pay them to anyone until they had further instructions from their new landlady herself, but to keep the money for rents and fines in their own possession until she told them precisely where to pay it. This was a point of special importance in view of what had happened about the Yorkshire property. Her cousin had garrisoned Skipton Castle on behalf of the King, and by the time of his death in December 1643 it had been besieged, or at least blockaded, for a year. King Charles had issued a warrant to Sir John Mallory to collect some of the rents and use them for the expenses of the garrison, so there was nothing to be hoped for from that quarter. The siege went on for the first two years of Lady Anne's undisputed ownership, the castle being eventually surrendered in 1645, just before Christmas Day.

By that time, she had arranged for a Mr. Edmund Pollard to collect the Westmorland rents of her behalf, and she wrote to Sir John Lowther to tell him so. The arrangement proved to have its own difficulties, however, and by the autumn of 1646 there were objections from some of the tenants round about Kirkby Stephen and

Stainmore. They were claiming rebates and exemptions which she did not recognise, and assigning grounds of hardship which she was in no position to verify. She had never faltered in her love for Westmorland and her tenants there, but when she was unable to judge matters in person she could do no more and no less than claim what was allotted to her by law, and that was that. In all essentials it was the answer she had given to King James and everybody else. 'Retain your loyalty, preserve your rights' is supposed to have been Lady Anne's motto, and certainly expresses her unfaltering, uncompromising principle. Those words are still to be read on the pedestal of the High Cross at Appleby, where they were engraved in the 18th century as an exhortation to the citizens of that ancient borough to stand firm against ineptitude in high places.

The trouble was, very largely, due to the sheer passage of time. Lady Anne had grateful and lively memories of the tenants who had welcomed her in her few weeks at Brougham and had appealed to her later on for her protection and support in their lawsuits, but those memories were some 30 years old by this time, and a new generation had grown up, of tenants who had never seen her and were not so likely to welcome her when they did. That was the position as it appeared to her in 1646, and it seems to have been largely symbolised by the triptych at Appleby. She had come into her inheritance at last, after all those years in which she might have done so much for it, and now she was old, and the fruit was rotten on the tree.

The tenants, on their side, had a sense of grievance against fate in general. The death of a landlord meant the end of a tenancy; the tenant who wished to continue in possession must apply to the new landlord for a renewal, and must pay a fine for it. They had had to do this on the death of Lady Anne's uncle in 1641, and now, only two years later, they had another change of landlord and must renew their tenancies all over again. It was something, naturally, to be told not to pay in a

Uncle in 1641
Cousin in 1643

hurry, in case they should be paying to the wrong person, but in the course of time the specific instructions came. Lady Anne had named and appointed her agent, and they were expected to pay what was due. The natural instinct was to avoid payment if it could be managed; to plead hardship, or special circumstances—such as that the countryside was full of Scots and soldiers—or simply the ancient argument, as old as the days of Rehoboam, that the previous terms had been too strict, and it was time for the custom to be reconsidered. But where the landlord was an unwilling absentee, and in no position to weigh such considerations on the spot, it was neither politic nor indeed possible to grant concessions blindfold, and the only thing to do at this stage was to abide by the existing agreement. Revisions might be considered later, but this was not the time for them.

In July 1647 her younger daughter, the Lady Isabella Sackville, was married to the Earl of Northampton in the church of Clerkenwell, where her mother and grandmother had lived for many years. Lady Anne herself was not present, she records, 'for manie reasons'. The political situation seems likely to have been one of them. Lord Pembroke's friendship with the King had not been entirely cancelled by his support of the parliament; it was he who had been sent to Newcastle to convey to Charles the Parliament's terms for peace, and when these had been rejected, and the Scots, on the other hand, had agreed to withdraw across the Border on settlement of their claims for pay and expenses, it was Pembroke again who went up to Newcastle, took over the person of the deserted King and brought him down to Northamptonshire for a period of not-too-rigorous detention at Holmby House. This action of the parliament gave offence to the more fanatical Independents of the army, some of whom upheld reform doctrines that parliament regarded, not unreasonably, as revolutionary and seditious. Parliament tried to counter this by disbanding the army without the back-pay due to it for winning the Civil War. Cromwell stoutly opposed this as being manifestly unfair, but he had no sympathy with the army extremists, and in consequence he was unpopular with both sides. When he ultimately decided to throw in his lot with the army, he saw that he must not let parliament counter this by setting up the King to oppose him, and in consequence, at the beginning of June, Cornet Joyce was sent down to Holmby, with a troop of horse for his authority, and removed King Charles peacefully but firmly under Pembroke's care.

There was no saying what might happen next. The army authorities were drawing up terms of agreement that might well prove attractive to the King. Pembroke might equally well be blamed by his colleagues, or by the London public, for letting him go too eassily, and it was not the time for his lady to go off to Clerkenwell and leave Baynard's Castle and its contents without a mistress, even for a day or two. On the other hand, the wedding had better take place as soon as possible, while the bride's stepfather (who resented it) had other matters to occupy his mind. The important thing was that it should be done, and done quickly, so done it accordingly was, and noted in the appropriate place on the family portrait.

London in general stood for the parliament against the army; there was rioting in the City, and a month after the wedding Cromwell and Fairfax rode through London with 18,000 men and took possession of the Tower, his military headquarters being set up at Putney. A further complication, from the Pembrokes' point of view, was that in that year a great deal of the fabric of Wilton House was destroyed by fire, so that the Baynard's Castle property became all the more important.

The King was well treated by the army, and was lodged at Hampton Court, which he liked. The proposals made to him were attractive and advantageous, but he hesitated about accepting them, in case he might do better elsewhere. Suddenly he contrived to escape from Hampton Court to Carisbrooke Castle in the Isle of Wight, and there re-opened negotiations with the Scots, not fully realising that instead of setting parliament and the army at odds, this action had brought them into alliance against him.

Appleby Castle had had a Royalist garrison in it for the past three years, but this revival of the Civil War was disastrous for it. An army from Scotland, under the Duke of Hamilton, came down into England in accordance with the latest arrangement made with the King. Cromwell moved north and defeated it at Preston, and two months later, in October 1648, the Appleby garrison capitulated and the castle was duly 'slighted', being rendered unsuitable for military occupation. (It must have been about this time that Sir James Turner, the military writer, had the curious adventure which he mentions in his memoirs as taking place 'in a village about half a mile from Applebie', where he had his stockings stolen by mice on three successive nights, and in searching for them found a purse of gold.) Meanwhile, parliament had become apprehensive of the growing power of the army, and had opened independent negotiations with the King at Carisbrooke. Once again Charles listened, quibbled, hesitated and avoided coming to a decision, and lost his last chance by his refusal to commit himself. The army lost patience, Colonel Pride set a guard upon the House of Commons and denied entrance to his political opponents, and when Cromwell got back from his northern campaign he found a truncated 'rump of a Parliament' more or less amenable to his will. The King was brought from Carisbrooke to Hurst Castle and from there to Windsor; at the end of January he stood his trial for treason in Westminster Hall before a court which he refused to recognise, and on the 30th of the month a shocked crowd saw him meet his death with calmness and dignity at the hands of a masked headsman outside the Banqueting House at Whitehall. It was Lady Anne's 59th birthday.

That single stroke of the axe cut through many things for England and for individual English people. The unthinkable thing had happened, the anointed King, whom so many had fought and died to save, had gone to his own death in spite of all, and his son, not yet 19, was out of the country, with no certainty that he would ever return. There was no cause left to fight for, the best course was to mind one's own business and put up, as patiently as might be, with whatever was to happen next. To Lady Anne it meant the end of the life she had known for nearly 50 years. There was no King to enjoy her allegiance, no ordered Court life to claim her attendance, no standards of dignity and decorum for her to uphold by her example. And, above all, there was no longer any reason to keep up the empty show of companionship with her husband. He had his grown-up sons, her own daughters were married now, and one of them had already made her a grandmother. She was not needed in London, nor wanted at Wilton; what was left of her life was her own at last, and she could do what she liked with it, and with her long-deferred inheritance of ruined towers and barren moorland pastures. Forty years and more ago, it might have been different, if she had succeeded when she should have done, and while her mother was yet alive to help her. Now there was no saying what it would be like, among houses that were neglected and tenants who were troublesome, but they were her own houses and her own people. Her sovereign was dead, her husband was estranged, she had no longer any obligations save those of her inheritance in the wilderness, so to the wilderness she went, and never came back.

It was on the 11 July 1649 that she left London for the north, travelling by easy stages, and on the 18th she arrived at Skipton, where she had been born. She had never set foot in it since she left it as a baby of 10 weeks old, and by order of the parliamentary authorities the castle had been rendered practically uninhabitable, so that she had to be quartered in the Long Gallery. Still, she was there at last, and after settling in she paid a visit to Barden Tower, which was still more ruinous, but of considerable importance to her at the moment because of its legal position. Her cousin, the last Lord Cumberland, had succeeded in getting it excluded from the bulk of the

Elizabeth Clifford

estate that must go by reversion to Lady Anne, and had
left it instead to his daughter, the Countess of Cork.
Lady Anne's view, however, was that the bequest was
invalid because, by her contention, it had never been his
to leave. Her father, she always claimed, had acted beyond
his powers in departing from the terms of the entail;
on his death the property had become hers, and nobody
else had any right to dispose of it. She was on pleasant
enough terms with Lady Cork, but to admit that claim
would be to abandon the contention that she had so
stoutly maintained, at such a cost, over so many years.
She would never do such a wrong to her principles, or her
ancestors, and she never did. Partly as a matter of principle, she spent a good deal of money on restoring the
place, went into residence there for some time in later
years, and made a point of urging any relatives who stayed
at Skipton to go over to Barden while they were there,
and see the building which had housed the 'Shepherd
Lord' and his descendants the first and second Earls
of Cumberland.

From Skipton she moved on, by way of Kirkby Lonsdale, to Appleby Castle, arriving there on 8 August, the
very day on which she and her mother had last left it
42 years before. After 10 days there, she went to
Brougham, thence in due course to Brough and the 'heape
of stones' that had been Pendragon, and to Skipton
again after a visit to Wharton Hall. In the new year she
was once again at Appleby, and it was there that she
learned of her husband's death in London on 23 January
1650. By the time she got the news of her second widowhood, she was just turned 60 years old.

Now, after so many years, she was independent. Her
daughters were both satisfactorily married, her grandchildren were arriving to carry on the line, she was no
longer an easy bait for fortune-hunters, and at last she
was in full possession of her patrimony. It was a far
cry from the gardens of Wilton and the great galleries
of Knole, and farther still from the masques and dances
at Whitehall when Inigo Jones designed the dresses, and

Ben Jonson wrote the songs, yet not so far, perhaps, from the days when little Anne Clifford had been 'much beloved' by a lonely, imperious, rather alarming old lady who bore on her back the responsibilities of a kingdom and showed no outward fear for any man. Early impressions, we are told, are never quite forgotten, and it was not in vain that some of Lady Anne's formative years had been spent in the shadow of the great Elizabeth.

At this point we are provided with a new source of information about her life and character. Nicolson and Burn, when they published their *History of Westmorland and Cumberland* in 1777, had owned, or had access to, a manuscript autobiography by George Sedgwick of Kendal, who had served her and her family for many years and wrote in 1682, only six years after her death. It is now untraceable, but the extracts which Nicolson and Burn embodied in their work are of great interest and value, and arouse a keen regret that the rest of the manuscript has not come down to us.

Its opening has a straightforward clarity foreshadowing that of *Robinson Crusoe*. We are told at once that Sedgwick was born in his father's house of Capplethwaite (near Kirkby Lonsdale) on 10 January 1618, that he went to school at Sedbergh, and owed much to the kindness of the headmaster, Gilbert Nelson, who took him into his own house as a boarder when his father lost money. He was sent to St. John's College in Cambridge, but could not afford to keep himself there for very long, and soon went on to join his father in London. It is here that Lady Anne first comes into the story. In the early years of her first marriage, when she and her mother were bringing a suit at York against her uncle Lord Cumberland, his grandfather Jeffrey Sedgwick had been one of the jurors, and had been noticed by them 'for true upright dealing'. The dowager Lady Cumberland had sent him a present of venison, with an appreciative letter and a gold ring inscribed with the appropriate motto 'Truth is crowned'. Now, apparently in 1634, Jeffrey's son brought his own son to Whitehall and sought an

audience of Lady Anne, by that time Countess of
Pembroke, in the hope that she might be able to do
something for the young scholar. She was much moved
at the sight of her mother's letter, and sent for Michael
Oldisworth, one of her husband's secretaries and her
own cousin, who was just then in want of a junior clerk.
Young Sedgwick was given the appointment and held it
for some four or five years, becoming secretary to Lord
Pembroke himself, and, on his death, to his son. The latter
was an unsatisfactory employer, and Sedgwick left him
after two years, whereupon Lady Anne dissuaded him
from accepting a post with a forthcoming embassy to
Turkey and took him into her own service as secretary
and agent. He served her faithfully for 18 years, and when
she herself was 80 she advised him to have an eye to the
future and see about getting a home of his own to which
he could retire when the time came. He found the still-
existing house of Collinfield, near Kendal: she gave
him £200 towards its purchase, and it was there, in the
tranquillity of retirement, that he wrote his autobiography
in 1682.

This document is the original source for most of the
legend that has grown up around the figure of Lady Anne
since her settling in the north. It is here that we read how
she found

> Skipton castle, that had been a stately building, scarce afford-
> ing lodging for herself and her family; so that she was resolv'd
> to build some lodging rooms in it, notwithstanding the
> malignancy of the times. Some gentlemen of the neighbour-
> hood, her friends and well-wishers, dissuaded her from it;
> alledging (and probably enough) that as fast as she built up,
> Oliver Cromwell would order it to be pulled down. She
> replied, If they do not take my estate from me, as long as
> I have money or credit, I will repair my houses, though I were
> sure to have them thrown down the next day. This being
> reported to Oliver,—Nay, says he, let her build what she
> will, she shall have no hindrance from me.
>
> Thereupon she began with Skipton castle, and in a year's
> time made it a very convenient house, though not so stately
> and large as it was before it was demolished.

As Sedgwick joined her service only a couple of years later, we may assume that he knew what he was talking about, though the major rebuilding carried out in 1657-59 tends to distract attention from the earlier work.

With her husband's death in 1650 her position became easier. When she left London in the previous summer, ready money had been hard to come by, and she had had to borrow £100 from the dowager Countess of Kent, leaving as security a bloodstone or 'heliotropian' cup (presumably the one which she later bequeathed to her eldest granddaughter, mentioning that it had belonged to her father, the Earl of Cumberland) and a little cabinet of crystal and silver-gilt. Now at last she was independent, a well-do-do widow with control of her own property, her two daughters married and well provided for, with neither king nor husband to command her allegiance. She had attained freedom and fortune after so many years, and was now to find out whether or not they were worth the waiting.

For a little while at first she could not be sure. A few weeks before Lord Pembroke's death she had arranged to pay Lady Kent her £100, and had sent a letter of thanks to her for her kindness. In a postscript she adds a message to 'the worthy Mr. Selden' (presumably John Selden, the jurist), saying how much relief she gets, in the midst of her troubles, from having 'excellent Chaucer's book' to turn to, and how, when she reads it, 'a little part of his beauteous spirit infuses itself in me', but the whole tone of the letter shows that she had a great deal to put up with. Her tenants were resentful, and she was unwelcome; her houses were ruinous, and she was uncomfortable. Her second husband had left her £500 worth of plate and linen, in addition to the personal jewellery that she had brought with her on her marriage, but a letter written in February to Christopher Marsh indicates that the executors were in a hurry to sell up the estate, so that he would have to take action at once with them to secure her legacy, or it would not be worth

having. Her cousin's daughter, Lady Cork, was suspected
of having designs on the London property—possibly in
retaliation for Lady Anne's own occupation of Barden
Tower—and there are signs that her younger daughter
and her husband were putting in claims for something
unspecified. Whatever it was that they wanted done,
Lady Anne writes that they are to have it, 'and then they
cannot blame me for it hereafter'. As so very often
happens, the interpretation of the will was causing a
certain amount of hard feeling between various members
of the family.

The trouble with the tenants took some years to settle.
The only thing she had to go by, at the outset, was the
strict letter of the tenancy agreements, and until she
could acquire personal knowledge and experience of local
conditions, she was in no position to forego what was
officially due to her. Some cases of hardship there might
be, but there would also be attempts to take advantage
of the newcomer's unfamiliarity, and it was impossible
for her, at this stage, to tell which was which. The only
thing to do was to leave the matter to the lawyers, even
though this involved a number of suits at law, some loss
of popularity and the expenditure of a good deal of
money. She was anxious to be a just and generous landlord, but she could not afford to grant rebates, or to
forego claims, until she knew, and her tenants knew, just
how she stood. Sedgwick tells us that Cromwell himself,
when Protector of the Commonwealth, followed King
James's example by trying to intervene as final arbitrator
in the affair, and appointed a commission of the local
gentry to consider the respective claims and wait upon
Lady Anne at Appleby to discuss them. When they came
there, he says,

> she used them with all kindness and courtesy, but told them
> plainly she would never refer any of her concerns in that kind
> to the protector or any person living, but leave it wholly to the
> discretion of the law; adding further, that she that had refused
> to submit to king James on the like account, would never do it to
> the protector, whatever hazard or danger she incurred thereby.

Later writers have been inclined to present the episode as an instance of indignant defiance by the staunch old Royalist, but Sedgwick's account—and he wrote while some of the commissioners were still living—shows it to have been something far more subtle. Neither she nor the commissioners, nor Cromwell himself, could be asked to go against the law, and it must be left to the professionals to decide what the legal position was. The argument was courteous, diplomatic and, in the circumstances, unanswerable.

Colonel Charles Fairfax, uncle of the Parliamentary general, proved to be a most helpful neighbour in relation to her affairs at Skipton, and in one letter to his nephew he sums up her attitude very clearly. She will show herself a generous and fair-minded landlord, he says, 'with such persons whose estates depend upon her award, if they have the good manners to acknowledge it her bounty'. Relaxation of the strict terms of a lease was not impossible, but it was to be enjoyed as a personal favour, not claimed impersonally as a right.

In the same way, it was not for tenants to waive any of their obligations as trivial or inconvenient, and Sedgwick tells us as much in his relation of another episode. The tenants were by no means all poverty-stricken farmers, but the leases had been drawn up in days when payment was taken not only in cash but in kind, usually oats and poultry—a very reasonable practice when the landlord came personally into the neighbourhood to receive his rents and could not always count on finding fresh provisions for himself, his attendants and all their horses. The story is worth recording in Sedgwick's own words.

There had been anciently paid for 400 years continuous, to the castle of Skipton, 800 boon hens yearly, and the like to the castle of Appleby, by the tenants, besides their rents. One Murgatroyd, a rich clothier of Hallifax, having bought a tenement near Skipton, was to pay one hen; which being demanded of him, he absolutely refused the payment of it. Her ladyship was resolved not to lose that hen, being

her ancient right, and the loss of all the rest depending upon
that. Being forced to bring an action against him at the
assizes, at York, she recovered the hen, though it cost her
200 *l*, and Mr Murgatroyd as much. And I believe Sir John
Otway and Sir Thomas Stringer got in fees in that cause
40 *l* each of them.

The root of the matter lies in the middle sentence, in the
two reasons ascribed to Lady Anne. Not only was it 'her
ancient right', a tradition that she respected and required
others to respect; its abandonment was a concession that,
if granted, might be reasonably demanded by all the rest.
On the one hand it meant the payment of one hen by
Mr. Murgatroyd; on the other, it might logically entail
the loss of 1,600 hens annually to Lady Anne. She won
her case, and it was well worth the money. The story
of her inviting Mr. Murgatroyd to dine, and having the
hen served up between them, has no contemporary authority, and would appear to be a piece of Victorian 'corro-
borative detail' in the manner of Pooh-Bah.

Meanwhile, she was turning her interests and activities
in another direction. She was a widow for the second time,
and it was fitting that she should do something for other,
poorer widows in the county of her inheritance. On the
last day of 1650 she bought a tract of land on the east
side of Boroughgate, and had it cleared for a new and
ambitious piece of work, the hospital of St. Anne. It
was to be an almshouse for 13 women of the neighbourhood who were too old and infirm to work any more for
their living, on the lines of a similar institution established
by Lady Cumberland in 1593 at Beansley. Hitherto her
main task, architecturally speaking, had been the repair
of her own living quarters after years of neglect or
deliberate damage. This time, however, an entirely new
building was to be designed and set up from the foundations, and on St. George's Day, 23 April 1651, she saw the
first stone of those foundations laid in her presence.

The building was, and is, a quadrangle of stone surrounding a central courtyard, and comprising a small
chapel, 12 little buildings for the individual Sisters, and

another, very slightly larger, for the senior one, who is called the Mother. The entrance gate is a reconstruction, and the living accommodation has been discreetly modernised, but the building still retains its original character and, very largely, its original appearance. The armorial bearings of Lady Anne and her Clifford and Vipont ancestors are displayed in boldly-carved stone escutcheons around the central courtyard, and the ground behind, looking down to the river is occupied by the Sisters' garden-plots. The general administration is in the hands of trustees, the owner of Appleby Castle always being one of them, and the vicar of Appleby normally acts as chaplain to the hospital and receives a small stipend for doing so. The Sisters draw a small allowance, live free of rent and rates and are governed by regulations which are substantially those laid down by Lady Anne more than 300 years ago.

Appleby Castle itself came in, at this time, for a certain amount of repair, but here the work was hindered by unavoidable difficulties. Though one King Charles was dead, his 21-year-old namesake and successor was now active in Scotland and was soon to be crowned at Scone. The Civil War was not over; parliament found it necessary to keep a considerable force of troops in the neighbourhood of the Border, and some of them were quartered at Appleby, so that Lady Anne, when in residence, found herself sharing her castle with a parliamentary garrison. Her difficulties became legendary in the countryside. Some years ago the present writer was told by a local garage employee, as a matter of unquestioned history, how she had sat in Appleby Castle, with the keys under her hand, and confronted Oliver Cromwell himself when none of her servants dared to face him, and that the great Protector had retired discomfited and respectful. The story was received discreetly and non-committally, as having no historical justification whatever, but Bishop Rainbow's funeral sermon tells us of an episode in which it may have originated. The Roundhead general in question was not Cromwell, but Harrison, the regicide, described by

Rainbow as 'one whom even his great Master himself
looked upon as under a Dispensation, more terribly
phanatical than any in his Host, terrible even to himself
and his usurped Power'. He quartered himself in her castle,
suspected her of sending assistance to the young King,
and 'being not able to make proof of that, he would
needs know her opinion, and dispute her out of her
Loyalty, at a time when she slept and lived but at his
mercy, giving her Alarms night and day when he listed'.
She might have temporised and expressed some measure
of agreement, and would have needed no excuse for doing
so, but she

> would not so easily yield, but would be superior in the Dis-
> pute, having Truth and Loyalty on her side, she would not
> betray them at the peril of her life and fortune; but boldly
> asserted, that she did love the King, that she would live and
> die in her Loyal thoughts to the King, and so with her courage
> dulled the edge of so sharp an Adversary, that by God's
> merciful restraint he did her no harm at this time.

The tension was less acute after the young King's defeat
at Worcester in 1651 had put an end to any immediate
risk of rebellion in the Royalist cause. Two years later,
Cromwell assumed supreme power, and meanwhile,
through the years, Lady Anne's rebuilding programme
went steadily on. Castle after castle was rendered serviceable as a residence if not as a fortification; the work at
Skipton was elaborated and the restoration of the castle
at Appleby was followed by those of Brougham, Brough
and even little Pendragon, which had lain ruined and
desolate for over 100 years. Between the major castle-
schemes, other works were taken in hand. St. Lawrence's
church in Appleby was repaired and restored in 1655,
and St. Michael's four years later. The hospital of St.
Anne had its first inmates appointed in 1653, the Mother
being the widow of Gilbert Nelson, the schoolmaster of
Sedbergh who had been such a good friend to Sedgwick
in his boyhood. His grateful pupil welcomed the chance
of recommending the appointment, and mentions at
the same time that Lady Anne took Mrs. Nelson's

daughter into her own service. Skipton church had been among the first she rebuilt, and the churches or chapels at Barden, Brougham, Mallerstang and the famous Nine-kirks—the church of St. Ninian at Brougham—were all repaired in greater or less degree. The Countess's Pillar, a stone column carrying a vertical sundial and adorned with escutcheons of the arms of Clifford and Russell, was set up in 1654 to mark the site of her last parting with her mother on the roadside near Brougham Castle, and two years later, on the 40th anniversary of the episode, she instituted an annual bequest of bread and money to the poor of Brougham, the distribution being made on a flat stone still to be seen hard by.

All these were works of piety and charity, as Rainbow points out in his sermon, but he makes a further point that is not always remembered. This extended programme was itself a benefaction to the people of Westmorland, because it provided employment for countless labourers, 'by which she did set the poor on work, thus curing their idleness, as well as supplying their indigency'. The strict landowner, insisting on her rights, was at the same time a provider of work and payer of wages, and a strange but increasingly familiar figure as she travelled from castle to castle or 'made the poor her pioneers' by hiring guides to lead her horse-litter over the tortuous bridle-paths where no coach would go. She could no longer be regarded as a remote, nebulous oppressor, someone whose only link with her people was the unrelenting exaction of her rents; she was the great lady who might be seen riding the bounds on her white horse, with a host of the nobility and gentry in attendance as if she were a queen, she was the patroness who seldom sent for anything from London, but bought her fabrics and provisions locally from her tenants and neighbours, and saw to it that they were paid in cash. Every Monday morning, when she was in residence, 20 poor householders of the neighbourhood received a small payment of money, and there was always something for the hungry who came to her gate. More than 30 years had gone by since the days when she had visited her mother at Brougham, there were not may left who remembered her as she had been, but she had come home at last, and the new generation was learning to know her now.

Chapter Eleven

THE OLD WASTE PLACES

The castle's gently render'd
Macbeth, V, vii

IN 1652 LADY ANNE started an autobiography based on her memories, diaries and other documents. For many years she had been compiling a genealogical history of the Vipont and Clifford families, based on her mother's researches and embodying transcripts of official records and other documentary evidence, taken originally in the course of her campaign to establish her daughter's rights. Now it was fair-copied in triplicate in three sets of three great folio volumes for the instruction and edification of Lady Anne and her two daughters, and adorned with genealogical trees and careful drawings of seals, badges, and armorial bearings. The material collected by Lady Cumberland is supplemented by details of Lady Anne's own formal claims for her inheritance, and followed by a passage described as 'a summary of the records, and a true memorial of the life of mee, the Lady Anne Clifford'. The copying has been done by a number of different secretaries and attendants, and checked and annotated by Lady Anne herself for the benefit of posterity.

The trouble about this last portion is that it *is* a summary and no more. Its value is undeniable, but its extreme compression reduces it, in a great degree, to a list of journeys undertaken and visitors entertained, and arouses a feeling of deep regret that the writer's original diary or 'day-by-day' book has not come down to us for comparison with this rather frigid epitome. The Knole diary has shown us how expressive a writer Lady Anne could be; this summary is a congested array of facts without the seasoning of the writer's feelings. These are indicated only by the near-statistical quality of many

entries, notably those recording anniversaries, coincidences
and visits from newly-acquired descendants. When Lady
Thanet, once 'the child' of Knole, came with four of her
younger children to Skipton in 1663, her mother notes
they came

> about eight o'clock at night into the chamber where I then
> lay, and wherein I was born into the world, and I then kissed
> them all with much joy and comfort, it being the first time
> that I saw my Daughter of Thanet, or these four younger
> Sonnes of hers in Skipton Castle, or in Craven, for it was the
> first time that they had ever come into Craven.

It is expressive, and it still shows the workings of the old
lady's mind, but we miss the fascinating trivialities and
irrelevances that make the earlier diary such a very moving
document. This summary is not a spontaneous expression
of feeling, but a selection of facts and emotions judiciously
recorded in tranquillity long after the event.

This period of residence in Skipton and the north,
established at last in her own ancestral property, ruling
her tenants and entertaining her neighbours and her
descendants, was something that at one time she had
given up hope of enjoying, but it had come after all,
and lasted for a quarter of a century. The first 10 years
or so were overshadowed by the disapproving rule of the
Protectorate, and now and again her castles were garrisoned by Roundhead troops in case of possible revolt,
but she went on practically unmoved. Castles and
churches, many of them dilapidated and near to ruin,
were repaired and set in order by local labour and made
to become, as far as possible, what they had been. There
was no sweeping change to Palladian elegance, no reflection of Wilton or imitation of Jones or de Caus; new
buildings, such as the stables and almshouses at Appleby,
were plain, graceful and efficient, while those old ones that
were slipping into decay were restored as nearly as possible
to their earlier form. Now and then there were alterations,
but they were not many, nor were they conspicuous. To a
great extent, Lady Anne chose to live and to worship after
the manner of her forefathers.

This, at times, must have had its difficulties. The services of the Church of England, and the use of the book of Common Prayer, were prohibited by law, but the old lady ignored the prohibition, and Sedgwick notes that she had the forbidden service held 'in the worst of times . . . duly in her own private chapel, where she never failed to be present at it, though she was threatened with sequestration: Yet by means of her honourable friends and relations in both houses of parliament she always escaped it'. Williamson's statement that 'she carried with her in her progresses her own chaplains, and they frequently officiated for her and her household' is directly contradicted by that of Bishop Rainbow, who was in a better position to know, and who says that she had in effect six domestic chaplains, *because* 'at every one of her Houses the Parochial Minister did officiate to her Family, as well as at their Cures, and they wanted not all due encouragements from so good a Patroness'. In each of her estates it was the same. By instinct or design she was no visitor from a remote life elsewhere, but the tradesmen knew her as a familiar customer, the various incumbents as a parishioner. Her very clothes were made locally. A few pages remain from an Appleby account book of 1673, and include the information that William Marshall, a tailor of Bongate, made her a black cloth gown for 39s. 6d., and Sedgwick tells us that 'a petticoat and waistcoat of black searge was her constant wear, nor could any persuade her to wear others'.

More than half a century had gone by since the time when she danced at Whitehall in costumes designed by Inigo Jones, or got Lady St. John's tailor to make her dresses of sea-green satin or green damask embroidered with gold. Now she was her own mistress and could wear what she liked; there was no one to find fault with her 'for wearing such ill clothes' as certain people had done in the past, and she had no objections to the plain fact that her two attendant gentlewomen habitually dressed much better than she did. Everyone who knew her could see that, and Rainbow summed up the position very neatly in her funeral sermon when he spoke of 'her Dress, not disliked by any, yet imitated by none'. There was no longer any need to follow the fashion, she had seen the court of Elizabeth change to that of King James, and in turn to the very different court of King Charles, and what fashionable society might be wearing in London was no longer any concern of hers. 'None disliked what she did, or was', says the bishop, 'because she was like herself in all things', and that was enough. He makes a shrewd reference to the *'semper eadem'* motto of Elizabeth I, 'whose Favour in Her first, and that Queen's last years, she was thought worthy of, and received', and indeed, in that remote countryside, it was not impossible, or indeed unnatural, to find a characteristic Elizabethan living on, unchanging in herself, yet admitting the possibility of change in others, well into the reign of Charles II.

She had been just over 10 years in the north when that king came to his own again, and for the last time Lady Anne took part in a spectacular public function. Appleby had been rigidly Royalist throughout the interregnum, despite the Roundhead garrisons in the castle and the 'constant sufferings, sequestrations and imprisonments' which the neighbouring gentlemen underwent for their loyalty to the King. Nicolson and Burn cite the narrative of the Reverend Thomas Machell, who tells how no one could be found to read aloud the proclamation declaring the dead king's son to be a proscribed traitor.

> The mayor withdrew himself, and the bailiffs (whose office it was) threw up their commissions, though but poor men, insomuch that the soldiers were glad to have recourse to a fellow in the market, an unclean bird, hatched at Kirkby Stephen, the nest of all traytours, who proclaimed it aloud, whilst the people stopped their ears and hearts, having nothing open but their eyes, and those even filled with tears . . . And the townsmen were not far behind this gallant example of their noble leaders; who when captain Atkinson came down from the castle with his musketeers to chuse a Roundhead mayor, and clapped his hand on his sword, saying, *I'll do it by this,* yet made resistance, for they then conferred

the office (to prevent bloodshed) on a moderate man, who had acted on neither side, except in bearing that office before, and so he was mayor two years together.

There was not always a parliamentary garrison at mayor-making time, so this particular crisis does not seem to have been repeated, but Cromwell later granted a charter of his own to the borough, through this same Atkinson's instrumentality. Another moderate man (Lancelot Machell, father of Thomas the narrator) refused to take office while this charter was in force, and when elected at the Restoration, he would not take the oath of office until he had sent for the document, cut it up with his own hands and thrown the pieces to a group of tailors to make into tape-measures, with the punning remark that 'it should never be a *measure* unto him'. Thomas Machell, as a boy of 14, was almost certainly an eye-witness of the festivities on the new King's coronation day,

> when there was almost as many bonefires as houses, and two stately high scaffolds at each end of the town, hung with cloth of arras and gold; whither, after service done at the church, the countess of Pembroke, with the mayor, aldermen and all the other gentry of the county ascended, with I know not how many trumpets, and an imperial crown carried before them, where they proclaimed, prayed for, and drank the health of the king upon their knees; the aged countess seeming young again to grace the solemnity. The expences of that day were very considerable. For throughout the town was kept open house, after the example of that noble countess, who thought not her gates then wide enough to receive her guests, which before had been too wide for receiving armies of soldiers.

Lady Anne was then in her 72nd year, and Machell's phrase is expressive enough for one to wonder what she looked like. This was no occasion for a black serge dress made locally, yet it was hardly possible to have something made to measure for this occasion when it was not likely to be worn again. A more recent episode provides a possible explanation. Shortly after the end of the Second World War, when clothing was still rationed and coupons were needed for dress material,

a very old and very great lady asked to see a dress and
hat which she had sent to a museum some years before.
They were duly sent over for inspection, and a few days
later she spoke of the costume to an official of the
museum, saying, 'That dress, you know. I felt I should
like to see it again, and I found to my surprise that I
could still get into it, so I thought I'd keep it. You don't
mind, do you?—I'll give you another instead'. Which
was duly done; the earlier dress was given some slight
modifications and worn at an important public function,
and looked magnificent.

Even so may it have been with Lady Anne. The little
lead coffin in the vault, still remembered by persons
I knew, shows that she did not grow stout in her old
age; its whole length is just under five feet, and it is
clear that at the end of her life she would still have been
able to wear the dresses of her girlhood. She was not
one to throw anything away prematurely; the gown
of 'sea-water green satin' of 1617 was apparently available to be painted in 1646, and it, or one of its fellows,
might still be laid up at Appleby or Brougham, in one
of the 'seaven or eight old truncks' mentioned in her
will as usually standing in her bedroom or in the room
next door. They contained 'for the most part old things
that were my deare and blessed mother's', but it is to
just such a receptacle that Lady Anne would be likely
to turn when she wanted something decorative at short
notice, that had been made to her measure by a good
tailor. It was old-fashioned, but not exaggeratedly youthful in cut, so there would be no suggestion of mutton
dressed as lamb.

Her own 'true memorial' of her life makes no mention
of this episode, recording only that on 23 April King
Charles was crowned at Westminster 'for which God be
praised', and that she herself was in Appleby at the
time. There does not seem to be any justification for
Williamson's statements that 'she sent up her page
Lancelot Machell, then 16 years old, to London, on this
occasion, to take some part in the ceremonial on her

behalf' and that 'his uncle acted as her page 36 years before at the Coronation of Charles I'. Lancelot Machell, Appleby's Restoration mayor, was never Lady Anne's page, though his daughter, Susan, became one of her gentlewomen, his brother, Henry, her house steward, and his youngest son, Lancelot, born about 1650, attendant, at the end of her life, to Thomas Strickland, receiver of her rents. In his will he leaves to his son and grandson (yet another Lancelot) and their descendants a silver portrait-medal of the Countess of Pembroke, given him 'as a token of her love, also another large medal being the picture of Charles II also given to me by the Countess, to remain in the evidence chest as monuments of her favour for ever'. As for the other allegation, Lancelot had no Machell uncle, his father having been an only son, and Lady Anne is unlikely to have been summoned to the coronation of Charles I, with a page or without one, as at that time she was recently widowed, was no longer Countess of Dorset, but Countess Dowager, had lately recovered from smallpox and was very self-conscious about what it might have done to her appearance. The omission of any reference to the performance on coronation night gives another pointer to the nature of the 'true memorial' and the character of its compiler. She had reached a stage when she no longer needed to record her feelings and actions in detail, so as to justify them, if necessary, to those who should come after her.

But, quite unexpectedly, the old lady was enjoying herself. After years and years of anxiety and frustration she had come into her own, and it was not dust and ashes after all. She had lands, and houses, and descendants, and they all needed looking after in one way or another, and, quite possibly to her surprise, she liked it. Popular imagination has been inclined to picture her as an autocratic and terrifying old person with a caustic tongue, but this appears to be the result of a certain amount of wishful thinking. The brusque and discourteous letter attributed to her by Horace Walpole

in 1753 has long been discredited as an 18th-century
fabrication, and the story of her saying she would not
come to the court of Charles II unless she might wear
blinkers is customarily repeated with the point left out,
and cited as an example of intolerant puritanism. The
Court of Charles II could have little to shock or surprise
anyone old enough to have lived in that of James I, and
the character and habits of her two husbands had taught
her much about the infinite variety of mankind. She
had been 10 years away from the metropolis and had
not kept in touch; she knew that there would necessarily
have been changes in fashions and ideas, and that she
would find much that was different without knowing
why. Bishop Rainbow tells how the suggestion was made
to her by a neighbour, but that when

> the Lady wished that she would once more go to London,
> and the Court, and glut her eyes with the sight of such happy
> Objects, and after that give up herself to her Country retire-
> ment; She suddenly, and pleasantly replyed, if I should go to
> those places, now so full of Gallantry and Glory, I ought
> to be used as they do ill-sighted, or unruly Horses, have
> Spectacles (or Blinkers) put before mine eyes, lest I should
> see and censure what I cannot competently judge of; be
> offended myself, or give offence to others.

She was apprehensive, not of being shocked, but of being
unwarrantably critical—or, quite simply, bored—and her
answer echoes that which the great lady of Shunem gave
to the prophet in rather similar circumstances: 'I dwell
among my own people'.

There was no doubt, by now, where her heart lay,
and she had made arrangements, by this time, for her
body to lie there likewise after death. In 1654 she had
had a burial-vault made for herself in the north-east
corner of Appleby church, and in the following year
an altar-tomb had been set up immediately over it, against
the northern wall of the Sanctuary. Behind the plain slab
of black marble rises a panel displaying the armorial
bearings of the ancestors from whom she derived her
inheritance, and the marriages from which in turn she

derived her blood. The arms of her uncle and cousin are not there. she is shown as the daughter of her father, and the whole display is an epitome of her inheritance in the direct line from that Vipont to whom the property had been granted in the first year of King John. The inscription on the front, setting out her name and titles, was cut in her lieftime, and probably under her supervision, and it is still possible to see a slight difference in the lettering of the last few lines, added some 20 years later to give particulars of her own death.

Much of her rebuilding, here as elsewhere, must have involved the replacement and re-pointing of existing material rather than the erection of anything new. In many places where the mortar was gone and the walls were crumbling and unsafe, it would be necessary to take off the roof and so many courses of the stonework as were loose, and set them back firmly bedded in new mortar, but as far as possible in their old positions, using as much of the original material as had not actually disintegrated. That explains at once her adherence, in churches and castles, to what some might consider an out-of-date style, and the difficulty of reconciling the contemporary statements that Appleby church was in great part 'taken down and rebuilded', and Bongate church 'raised out of its ruins' with the amount of medieval material still to be seen in both. Certain alterations, of course, there were; a vestry on the north side of the chancel at Appleby was removed, and a small private transept, on the south of the Sanctuary, was turned into an extension of the south aisle by the removal of a dividing wall, while the stability of both Appleby and Bongate churches was safeguarded by the provision of reinforcing buttresses, but on the whole, Lady Anne's restorations interfered very little with the design of the earlier builders.

To her time, and almost certainly to her bounty, must be ascribed the panels of the royal arms once seen in both churches. The panel at Appleby surmounts a passage from the book of Isaiah (xxxiii, 15 and 17) that suggests it was set up in 1660 or 1661 in honour of the restoration

or coronation of Charles II, while that at Bongate specifically bore the date of the latter year. King Charles, who
had no illusions about his personal appearance, might
have grimaced at the promise that 'thine eyes shall see
the king in his beauty', but the loyalty of the whole
passage was unquestionable. More felicitous, perhaps, was
another passage, from the same prophet, to which Lady
Anne refers on the inscribed tablets that she caused to
be set up in more than one of her repaired castles, recording the dates of her work of restoration:

> And they that shall be of thee shall build the old waste
> places; thou shalt raise up the foundations of many genera-
> tions, and thou shalt be called, The repairer of the breach,
> The restorer of paths to dwell in. (Isaiah, lviii, 12.)

The barren lands were being encouraged to bear again,
the last heiress of the great line of Clifford had lived to
look on her children and grandchildren and great-
grandchildren, she had gone over ways 'where never
coach went before', and had won the respect and affection of those about her, from the country landowners
who came to wait upon her on her formal Progresses
to the 'ancient maids' in her almshouses and the poorest
cottagers who guided her horse-litter along the rude path-
ways of the fells. She had waited long, and endured
much, and had come to her long-delayed inheritance at a
time when she thought her life was practically over, but
it had proved to be nothing of the kind, for her continued
works of repair and restoration and benefaction were
awakening feelings that she had once thought atrophied
for ever, and bringing life to the old waste places of her
much-enduring heart.

Chapter Twelve

QUIET POSSESSION

Thou thy worldly task hast done;
Home art gone, and ta'en they wages.

Cymbeline, IV, ii

SHE LIVED TO BE 86, and Sedgwick and Rainbow between them give a very clear indication of her life and character in her latter years. Rainbow makes it plain that in spite of her unquestionable authority she was not intolerant nor censorious. She knew what she wanted, and made sure that she got it, but there was no insistence that it was the only way of life for anyone. She had come into her own, and was doing what she liked with her own, but had no desire to impose her particular way of life on other people if their tastes lay in other directions; in his expressive phrase, she was 'strict and straitlac'd, as to her self; but benign, candid, and favourable, leaving others to their Liberty.

As increasing age made it impossible for her to ride about her property as she used to do, she settled down into a way of life that was physically less energetic but mentally no less active than of old, and still conducted after the Elizabethan manner. Whether she were at Skipton, Appleby, or Brougham, the routine was the same. She herself kept to her own room, and had her meals there, where relatives or specially favoured guests were sometimes invited to join her. As a general rule, guests were entertained to meals by her chief officers in a neighbouring room—at Brougham, we know, it was the room called the Painted Chamber—and joined her for conversation in her apartment after the eating and drinking were over and the dishes had been cleared away. The household in general dined in almost

collegiate fashion at their appropriate tables in the Hall.
Once again we may turn to the funeral sermon for an
expressive summary:

> She was absolute Mistris of her Self, her Resolutions, Actions,
> and Time; and yet allowed a time for every purpose, for all
> Addresses, for any Persons; None had access but by leave,
> when she call'd; but none were rejected; none must stay
> longer than she would; yet none departed unsatisfied. Like
> him at the Stern, she seem'd to do little or nothing, but
> indeed turn'd and steer'd the whole course of her Affairs.

This posthumous tribute is corroborated, and thus
rendered still more valuable, by the existence of a few
pages of Lady Anne's diary in the last months of her life,
showing us the sytem in action. On New Year's Day 1676,
for instance, Mrs. Winch called to see her from Seatree
Park, 'so I had her into my chamber and kissed her, and
she dined without with my folks in the Painted Room,
and after I had her again into my chamber and talked
with her a good while, and I gave her four pairs of Buck-
skin Gloves that came from Kendal'. The old lady was
accustomed to retire early by this time, as she mentions
that she was in bed when Allan Strickland, her chief
steward, so far forgot himself as to 'comitt some disorder
in my house' at seven o'clock that evening—presumably
by taking too much to drink as it was New Year, and a
Saturday night at that. She was not told of it at the time,
but it was duly reported to her next morning by her
sheriff, and on the culprit's appearing properly contrite
she 'was moved upon his ingenious acknowledgement
and confession to pardon him'.

Entry after entry contains the line 'I went not out of
the House nor out of my Chamber to-day'—which, in view
of her age, and the time of year, is not surprising—but
that upper room in the gatehouse at Brougham was still
the centre of activity of the whole castle, and indeed of
the whole estate. She dictated letters, she received visitors,
she read the appointed psalms for the day, she interviewed
tradesmen, sometimes with shrewd criticism, and super-
vised the paying of household bills, and on Sundays and

Wednesdays Mr. Grasty, the parson of Brougham, came in to hold a short family service of prayer. Every few weeks she pared the nails of her fingers and toes and carefully burnt the parings, as she did with the clippings when she had her hair cut—a relic of ancient superstition, that considered it unsafe to risk letting any part of one's anatomy get into someone else's hands in case it should be used for witchcraft. When she was arranging for her household to take communion, as she did four times in the year, she would prepare them for it by buying and distributing little books of devotion, taking care, Rainbow tells us, 'that every one might take their choice of such Books as they had not had before'.

Besides this distribution of religious reading to her household, she was fond of giving little personal presents to the visitors who came to see her. Gloves, lace ruffles and small sums of money are noted in the diary of her last months, and the few pages remaining from her 1673 account book. There are entries recording the purchase of gloves, ruffles, books of devotion (from a clergyman in Kirkby Stephen), and lengths of linen cloth from Kendal and bone-lace from 'the deafe woman of my almshouse here at Appleby', all marked 'to give away'. Larger presents were wooden stock-locks, usually bearing the initials A.P., for Anne Pembroke, like the one still in position at Appleby Castle. There is one at Great Asby rectory, traditionally commemorating her having taken shelter there from a sudden storm, one that she gave to George Sedgwick is in his house at Collinfield, by Kendal, and there is yet another, obviously a gift to Rainbow, at Rose Castle, the palace of the Bishops of Carlisle.

Other gifts by her were portraits, which appear for the most part to have been either head-and-shoulder copies of the full-length likeness in the triptych or, quite possibly, some of the painter's original studies for it. Some of them claim to represent her in extreme old age, but this is disproved by their very close correspondence with the triptych-portrait, painted when she was fifty-six. It seems likely that the later figure, in inscription or tradition, represents the age she had attained when she gave the picture to its recipient. The silver portrait-metal given to Lancelot Machell, and mentioned in his will, shows her dressed in very much the same style as the 1646 picture, and the crowned figure of Faith on the reverse, recalling Sedgewick's story of the motto on the ring,* suggests that she had had the medal struck in 1643 to commemorate her coming at last to her long-delayed inheritance and justifying her own and her mother's belief in the justice of her claim.

One visitor, in these last months of her life, was 'Elizabeth Atkinson daughter of Mr. Warcopp', who dined with others in the Painted Room and was afterwards received, kissed and given 2s. 6d. before she left. Dr. Williamson has very convincingly identified her with the widow of the Roundhead captain who had tried to influence the mayoral election by force of arms. After the Restoration he was involved in the Kaber Rigg plot against Charles II, was tried in Appleby Moot Hall for high treason at the assizes in 1664, and was duly hanged, drawn and quartered—tradition says, in the grounds of Appleby Castle. Lady Anne noted the trial in her diary, naming him as 'Robert Atkinson, one of my tenants in Mallerstange, and that had been my great Enemie', but it is said that his widow and children remained on their estate at Dalesfoot at a purely nominal rent, and it would seem that 12 years later Mrs. Atkinson might still be the recipient of the old Royalist's kindness.

The diary goes on, through February and March, with its record of visitors, household business, odd domestic payments and an increasing number of reminiscences of 60 years before. On 19 March she had 'a violent fitt of the wind, so that it caused me to fall into a swooning fitt for half an hour together', but she was well enough after dinner to receive two of her tenants and have the usual Sunday service held in her room. Next day she 'remembered how this day was 60 years did I and my blessed

*See page 149.

mother in Brougham Castle give in our answer in writing
that we would not stand to the award the four Lord
Chief Judges meant to make concerning the lands of
mine inheritance, which did spin out a great deal of
trouble to us, yet God turned it to the best'. On the
21st, the entry is only 'I went not out all this day', and on
the day after that, very quietly, she died. Sight and hearing
were failing her at the end, but she knew by heart, and
was heard repeating, the eighth chapter of St. Paul's
Epistle to the Romans, 'being', says Rainbow, 'the last
words of Continuance, which this dying lady spoke'.

By her will, signed at Pendragon Castle in 1674, she
left the Westmorland property to her elder daughter,
now the dowager Lady Thanet, and the Skipton property
to Alethea, daughter of the younger, Lady Northampton,
who had died in 1661. Grandchildren, great-grandchildren,
friends and old servants are enumerated in it and
bequeathed personal mementoes in the way of jewellery,
miniatures, pieces of plate or other property (the receiver
of her rents in Craven is to have 'fower of my best oxen'),
and her son-in-law, Lord Northampton, is to have 'six
of the best peices of my father's armors that he shall
chuse, hoping he will leave them to his daughter the
Lady Alethea Compton, my grandchild'. Her grandson,
Lord Thanet, and his brother John are to have 'the remain-
der of the two rich armors which were my noble father's
to remaine to them and their posterity (if they soe please)
as a remembrance of him'. The wording of this bequest
may account for the total disappearance of the armour
with the golden stars, illustrated in the Hilliard miniature
and the family portrait at Appleby. Even if Lord Northampton restricted himself to taking no more than six pieces
of that particular suit, the Tufton brothers would have
little use for what was left. The other armour, with its
magnificent engraved decoration, remained at Appleby,
and was sold in the present century to America. Northampton survived his daughter Alethea, so that his six
pieces would still be his own property at her death and
would not go back to the Tuftons with the rest of her

estate, and without them, whichever they were, the suit would be manifestly incomplete and unsuitable for display. Eventually it might be sold as scrap metal, as much armour was in the following century, or even buried somewhere to get it out of the way, as is said to have been done at Wilton in later years, but the splitting-up of that bequest may be reckoned as one of Lady Anne's few errors of judgement.

Another, perhaps, was the elaborate entail. The estates were willed to Lady Thanet's second son, John, and his heirs, and failing them, to his three younger brothers in succession. Last of all came the eldest grandson, Nicholas, Earl of Thanet, 'whom I now name in the last place, not for want of affection or good will in me towards him, but because he is now by the death of his father possest of a great inheritance in the southerne parts'. This entail was repeated in the will of Lady Thanet, who did not long survive her mother, and Lord Thanet then stepped in and claimed the estate over the heads of his younger brothers, as the eldest and indisputable heir. The wheel had come full circle, and he was using the very argument that his grandmother had put forward many years before, maintaining that like her father she had acted irregularly in leaving the property out of the direct line. Unlike Lady Anne, he was successful in his claim, and took over the inheritance to the exclusion of those brothers whom the will had named before him, but—also unlike her—he did not live to enjoy it long. He died in 1679, and his three younger brothers, John, Richard and Thomas, came into it in succession.

By this time Lady Alethea had also died, and her share of the inheritance had come back to the Thanets, who were more than ever 'possest of a great inheritance in the southerne parts'. The newest Lord Thanet had little use for so many castles in the north, and saw no reason to spend money on their upkeep. Appleby was at least a market town of some size and importance, and its castle would be the most suitable, therefore, to retain as an occasional residence, so it was drastically modernised in consequence, while the others were allowed, and encouraged, to fall into decay. Dressed stone was obtained by demolition at Brougham and Brough, and used to enlarge the residential portion at Appleby in a style more suited to the elegance of the approaching 18th century; timber, lead and fittings were sold off, Lady Anne's own additions and outbuildings were demolished as an easy source of miscellaneous building material for the neighbourhood, and while Appleby Castle was converted to an elegant residence for a person of quality, the other three had reverted to the state in which Camden had found and described Pendragon, 'which hath nothing left unto it unconsumed by time, besides the bare name, and an heape of stones'.

Time in turn was to consume the line of the Thanets; the last earl died unmarried in 1849, and now the identity and the very name of Westmorland are marked for extinction in the cause of governmental convenience. Yet folk-memory is long and loyal, and the dwellers on the Clifford estates—many of them still bearing the names of her officers and household servants—will continue to remember and honour the name of Lady Anne. Bishop Rainbow, preaching at her funeral in Appleby church, spoke with a sincerity that may excuse his momentary confusion of metaphor, when he said:

> Thus fell at last this goodly Building; thus died this great wise Woman; who while she lived was the Honour of her Sex and Age, fitter for an History than a Sermon.
>
> Who having well considered that her last Remove (how soon she knew not) must be to the House of Death, she built her own Apartment there; the Tomb before your eyes; against this day, on which we are all now here met to give her Reliques Livery and Seizin, quiet possession.
>
> And while her Dust lies silent in that Chamber of Death, the Monuments which she had built in the Hearts of all that knew her, shall speak loud in the ears of a profligate Generation; and tell, that in this general Corruption, lapsed times decay, and downfal of Vertue, The thrice Illustrious Anne Countess of Pembroke, Dorset and Montgomery stood immovable in her integrity of Manners, Vertue and Religion . . .

He was speaking for his own generation, or rather for that of his hearers, as he himself was nearly 70, but his words, and the truth behind them, have lasted longer than he knew.

INDEX